HOW TO ENJOY THE LOVE OF YOUR LIFE

Books by Harold H. Bloomfield, M.D.

HOW TO ENJOY THE LOVE OF YOUR LIFE

THE HOLISTIC WAY TO HEALTH AND HAPPINESS
(with Robert B. Kory)

HOW TO SURVIVE THE LOSS OF A LOVE
(with Melba Colgrove, Ph.D., and Peter McWilliams)

HAPPINESS: THE TM PROGRAM, PSYCHIATRY AND ENLIGHTENMENT
(with Robert B. Kory)

TM: DISCOVERING INNER ENERGY AND OVERCOMING STRESS
(with Michael P. Cain, Dennis T. Jaffe, and Robert B. Kory)

How to Enjoy the Love of Your Life

Over 100 Ways to Enrich Your Love Life

Harold H. Bloomfield, M.D.

Doubleday & Company, Inc., Garden City, New York 1979

ISBN: 0-385-14239-0
Library of Congress Catalog Card Number 77-27697

Printed in the United States of America

First Edition

For you, Cherylyn, with my love.

For my father, mother, sister, teachers, and friends, who helped form my Love,

For the Divine spark from whence it came.

CONTENTS

Author's Preface 8

LOVE 11

love's puzzlement / the search for love / loving is simple, right? / the signs and symptoms of romance / the letdown / love addiction / finding love / the magic of love / intimacy / the physical sensations of love / true love / love's components / giving / empathy / acceptance / respect / openness / honesty / pseudo-love / love is innocent / unconditional love / living love / the path to love.

GROWING 39

a loving birthright / well begun is half done / adolescent love / growing pains / emotional blocks to the flow of love / overcoming guilt / love thy self / a self-love checklist / pretense/defense / love's great dampener: chronic fatigue / the mask of depression / up from depression / your self-image / self-inventory / mirror, mirror on the wall / self-esteem building / health is your opportunity / the "sweet" life / fitness can be fun / stretching exercises / develop your person power / assertive training / afraid to love? / don juan syndrome / the practice of love / what we put attention on grows stronger / the expansion of happiness / r_x for dis-ease / a calm mind / the healing silence / when the need for psychotherapy? / the therapeutic process / guidelines for change / self-mastery / cultivate preferences / finding your dharma / love's labor / search for excellence / success / love blossoms in the soil of happiness / refined appreciation / attractiveness / the right model / self-actualization / the loving person / the world is as you are / birds of a feather flock together.

SHARING 101

staying in love / communication skills / effective listening / feedback / favor positivity / friendship / maleness/femaleness / your heart line / the ethics of love / timing / anaclitic and narcissistic love / the romantic urge to marry / marital readiness / selecting a partner / two halves don't make a whole / commitment / like "pillars of the temple" / marital style / happily ever after / chronic enjoyment / being-together / love, work, and play / freedom and jealousy / relationship crises / marital therapy / sensitivity training / nude dialogue / non-verbal exercises / massage / your love sanctuary / love's play / love vs. lust / sexual health / sexual dysfunction / sexual fantasy / x-rated, in-joy / multi-orgasm for two / spiritual love-making / tantra / conceived and received with love / love: the essential nutrition / freud was right / too much love? / the children of tomorrow / your family roots.

TRANSCENDING 163

the transcendent / gateway to love / love consciousness /guiding light / spirituality / are you a mystic? / spiritual crises / faith / put love first / the power of prayer / life after death? / higher consciousness / toward an enlightened you / integration of opposites / universal values / truth / the imprisoned splendor / creativity / beauty / nature / a million, million miracles / save our planet / wisdom / a loving education / devotion / service / brotherly love / justice / joyous simplicity / imagine! / a realized society / it could all begin with you / toward a new age / transformation at the speed of love.

BIBLIOGRAPHY 214

AUTHOR'S PREFACE

Welcome. Any number of reasons may have brought you to this book. The frustration of one love relationship after another, marriage not having lived up to its expectations, loneliness, emptiness, or the absence of joy in your life, feeling some contentment already but seeking more love, more joy—these experiences are becoming commonplace. In my psychiatric practice almost every person seen has voiced a deep longing to share with a fellow human being the words "I love you," in a meaningful and ongoing way. An unfulfilled love life is not only the complaint most often heard in a psychiatrist's office, but is truly pervasive today.

The title, *How to Enjoy the Love of Your Life,* has a double meaning, which is the theme of this book. When most people think of finding "the love of their life," a vision of a Prince Charming or a Charlie's Angel comes to mind. Literally millions are suffering disappointment in love, hoping, waiting for Mr. or Ms. Right to come along. This book is to change your life by actively improving your own well-being. It will help you to make a 180-degree turn, from looking for Mr. or Ms. Right out there, with ups, downs, and mostly frustration, to first becoming the right person, developing your full potential for love.

This book will detail more than one hundred ways for you to enrich your love life. The best of ancient and modern psychological thought has been incorporated for your use. There is a tremendous technology of human growth now available to help each of us become all that we are capable of becoming. We will begin with learning to truly love ourselves, healing our hurts and emotional wounds, then tapping our deeper reservoirs of care and compassion. To share love we must first have it. We will investigate a myriad of blocks to the flow of love—fear, guilt, loneliness, and depression—and the specific means for their alleviation. The reader will learn how to maximize love and joy in his or her relationships. Love, its components and manifestations, will be examined as will improving communication skills and marriage.

In all humility, this book is not meant to come up with something startling or revolutionary in regard to love and its cultivation. Despite the great tomes written on love, unhappiness and lack of love abound. The six o'clock news is reminder enough; dreary statistics need not be cited. We need to explore the importance of love and its cultivation, from classic sources and modern psychology, until we make love a systematic part of our lives, and those of our children.

A major step to learning to love and enjoy in a deeper way is first to recognize that there is no easy, magical means to a lasting and fulfilling love relationship. This book will not present a quick panacea for solving all your love problems. To do so would be to raise your expectations just later to leave you feeling disappointed. Panaceas are not the answer. A total, holistic approach is.

After we dispel the illusion of depending on romance alone as the quick, easy path to a lasting love, you will find that the real power for improved love relations lies mainly within you. You will be presented with guidelines and tools for growing, sharing, transcending—developing your full capacity for love. It is not as if you will read this book and next day magically turn into a Cinderella or Prince Charming. Rather you will be launched on an adventure, a process, of your heart unfolding. Read the book again from time to time. Many of the steps for expanding your love and joy will require determination and applying new skills. Remember, you can change, and the love within will guide you.

In writing this book, I have used third-person pronouns and collective nouns in the masculine gender. I ask the forgiveness of those readers who will find this offensive. The English language currently offers no suitable alternative that is not either too cumbersome or unwielding throughout, but especially when I discuss the self-actualizing and fully loving individual I have equally in mind the female and male of our species.

My intent is to have this book serve as a loving reminder to help instill more love and satisfaction into our lives. Toward this end a program of holistic development of body, mind, spirit, relationships, and environment is described. I offer this book to you the reader with my love, and hope that you will be pleased.

LOVE

—Love's Puzzlement
—The Search for Love
—Loving Is Simple, Right?
—The Signs and Symptoms of Romance
—The Letdown
—Love Addiction
—Finding Love
—The Magic of Love
—Intimacy
—The Physical Sensations of Love
—True Love
—Love's Components
—Giving
—Empathy
—Acceptance
—Respect
—Openness
—Honesty
—Pseudo-love
—Love Is Innocent
—Unconditional Love
—Living Love
—The Path to Love

LOVE'S PUZZLEMENT

- Afraid to love? Not even sure any more what love feels like?

- Is love an art? A pleasant sensation which one "falls into"? A quest?

- Is it, as Freud would have it, just "aim-inhibited sexuality"?

- Is your Prince Charming or Cinderella riding on a white horse . . . and no horses are allowed in your neighborhood?

- I love you . . . but . . . except that . . . if only . . .

- Is love an illusion that must crash on the hard rocks of "reality"? *Romeo and Juliet, Tristan and Isolde, West Side Story*—can a true love not survive in the harsh, cruel world?

- "I'm crazy about you," "I'm wild about her," "I'm madly in love" . . . (three weeks later) . . . "I hate you," "This is getting too heavy," "Fifty ways to leave your lover"—as in the song "Alfie," "What's it all about?"

THE SEARCH FOR LOVE

• Perhaps no experience is more common today than the frustration of trying to love or be loved.

• As an infant we are loved (hopefully) just because we exist—unconditional praise and care—and we spend the rest of our lives trying to recapture that state of wholeness, acceptance, and peace.

• Almost everyone secretly or explicitly expresses concern about his or her capacity to love.

• Problems centering around love are the most common complaint heard in a psychiatrist's office:

- —a housewife tells how much she has been trying to love her children, yet gets angry with them over trifles.
- —a married couple describe how hard they have been working to make each other happy, and later lament how frustrated and unhappy they are.
- —a student bemoans the futility of his efforts to find a girlfriend, feeling depressed and in despair.
- —an elderly mother's loneliness at the emptiness of her nest.
- —separation, divorce, and death—with the anger, despair, and emptiness they bring.

• Despite our failures, the search for love continues. "Having neither wife nor child, he became enamored of a large monkey" (Balzac). We all need someone to love; love is a very basic human need.

LOVING IS SIMPLE, RIGHT?

• Why is it that love gives rise to such soaring hopes and expectations and yet fails so regularly?

• Loving is simple, right? It's just finding Mr. or Ms. Right that is the problem. Then—finally—your dark night of the soul is ended, your depression is lifted: for your true love has appeared.

• When two people suddenly let down the barriers between them and "fall in love," this rush to intimacy can be one of the most thrilling and exciting experiences in life.

• It's easy, just waiting for our prince (or princess) to come: a beautiful dream, an exquisite fantasy, the ultimate happily-ever-after.

THE SIGNS AND SYMPTOMS OF ROMANCE

•There is a tendency to focus upon the beloved one to the exclusion of others. "The rest of the world could disappear," as long as the lovers can be together.

•The lovers have a special power, an animal magnetism. They may develop a private language, secret words, and gestures.

•The symptoms of romantic love:
- –Lightheartedness
- –Weakness
- –Chills
- –A pounding of the heart
- –A swelling in the chest
- –Frequent sighs
- –Rapid, shallow breathing
- –Butterflies in the stomach
- –Shaky legs
- –Goose bumps
- –Tingling, trembling

•Almost everyone has experienced the thrill, the rush, the excitement, the elation—of these symptoms of romance.

•Take another look. Amazingly, they are also the symptoms of anxiety.

•Excitement and anxiety have the same physiological components. In both cases, the body can keep the flow of adrenalin going for just so long before exhaustion, depression, or boredom ensue.

•Sexual attraction and consummation "up the ante" even more, to even higher levels of exhilaration and ecstasy.

THE LETDOWN

- Caught in a romantic whirl, the participants start making tremendous demands upon each other. Both believe they have finally found the one who will magically meet all their needs.

- When the newness and fanfare wears off and the initial excitement becomes difficult to sustain, illusions start bursting: one after the other.

- As the two people become well acquainted and "more real," the glitter wears off, causing disappointment and boredom. Soon you decide it's obvious you didn't choose the right person after all.

- Feelings are transitory, especially the romantic high of falling in love. The exhilaration is intense, for it looks as if your dreams are about to come true. But with disillusionment, it's time to move on.

- Your love life becomes a constant series of ups and downs. By its very nature, romantic love is transitory.

LOVE ADDICTION

•Look around. Look at your own life. What most of us call love is the intense exhilaration of falling in love. But then it becomes less and less intense and we grow disappointed.

•Soon the desire comes for a new conquest—a new Mr. Magic or Ms. Far-out, always with the illusion that the next one will be different, the one, the love of your life.

•Most people in the Western world are in search of lasting romantic love. No wonder there is so much disappointment in love, no wonder so many marriages fail. Relationships built on excitement alone are doomed to failure.

•Romantic love is not "bad"; indeed, it is a beautiful experience. But stars and rockets do not a lifetime make. Romantic love must give rise to a more mature loving. It is not an end in itself, rather a step along the way.

FINDING LOVE

•We can only give to one another that which we already have. One can give to the other only from what is most alive within one's being—joy, wisdom, and understanding.

•This flow of energy enriches the sense of aliveness in both people. Love is not something we force. It is a deep tender feeling we allow.

•Trying to fill an empty heart from the outside alone is like trying to fill a bottomless pit. Love is the great healing force . . . but we cannot just depend on a steady flow from the outside. Life is too full of vicissitudes and change.

•Your truest nature is love, but instead of seeking love within you have gone outside to find it. You have gone begging all around for that which you already own.

•Go to the source of your own being in your search for love. Deep within you there lies a non-changing source of love. You are not the giver of love nor the receiver of love: You are love itself.

THE MAGIC OF LOVE

•Love transcends the boundaries of our existence, soothes the pangs of separation.

•We would go mad if we could not reach out from the prison of our aloneness to unite with others and the world. Boundaries without the infusion of love's unboundedness would be an unbearable prison.

•Love transforms the mundane into the extraordinary. Childlike joy and spontaneity return. Paradise lost becomes paradise regained.

•Is this feeling neurotic, infantile, irrational? Is love merely an illusion? Romantic love must mature into a more permanent love structured in our awareness. It is a window, a vision of possibilities.

INTIMACY

- Intimacy comes in all sizes and shapes—each with its own special kind of pleasure.

- In our quick-snack, frozen-food consumer economy, the brand which is most special gets most frequently overlooked—the one that comes with time.

- Time not only for the relationship but time to become a fully healthy, happy, loving human being.

- Love is a growth process, for the individual, for the relationship. It is not something that reaches full maturity at once.

- A romantic whirl grows rapidly but can wither just as fast; intimacy grows slowly but endures.

THE PHYSICAL SENSATIONS OF LOVE

•Some people find it difficult to say "I love you" because they lack any bodily awareness of that emotion.

•"I love you" is often meant really as "I need you"—it is asking *for* love rather than an expression of a bodily state. The former is conditional—"I'll love you if you'll love me"; the latter is an unconditional expression of a bodily feeling that is already there.

•True love is experienced in the very center of one's being. This is the deepest feeling of love. It is felt in or about the heart, often extending out into both arms, up to the lips and head and down to the genitals (this is different from purely erotic love where the sensations arise from the genitals and may extend up toward the heart).

•It is the heart *chakra* (energy center) opening up, in the solar plexus of the chest, as is experienced sometimes by:

—Lovers during total orgasm
—Mothers during delivery or nursing
—Devotees of God during prayer

•To love is a discrete physical sensation, but it is also a

—Commitment
—Judgment
—Decision
—Way of life

TRUE LOVE

•True love comes from the essence of Being—from the I in me to the I in you.

•True love is the natural expansion of the joy of being alive. A classic misunderstanding held by most people is that they have to love or be loved *in order* to be happy. Indeed, the reverse is true. Happiness is the foundation as well as the result of loving.

•Love is like an ocean. Its great meaning is not to be found in the waves of excitement on its surface, but in the profound silence of its depths.

•The great truth about love is that it really makes less difference whom we love—*as long as we love.*

LOVE'S COMPONENTS

•Love is not just a subjective feeling, an emotion, but a series of actions which convey concern, involvement, and support. Love's components help distinguish passion, infatuation, and neurotic clinging from the genuine thing.

•Erich Fromm elucidated four basic elements common to all forms of love:

–Care
–Responsibility
–Respect
–Knowledge

•Love requires being able to transcend one's own boundaries, to truly feel what the other person is feeling, to delight in the other's growth.

•Real love means fully accepting another person, no strings attached. "I love you because I need you" is transformed into "I appreciate and value you for what you are."

•To disrespect, disapprove, scold, punish, ignore, reject, frustrate, discourage, or intimidate produces harm, damage, neurosis –these actions are unloving. To respect, value, like, protect, care, appreciate; to enjoy is the substance of being loving.

•Knowledge of yourself, the other, and loving is essential–and that is what this book is about.

GIVING

•Too many people are preoccupied with falling in love and being loved. If two people come together, each expecting the other to provide attention, service, and caring, both get caught up in taking. Both lose.

•The other person must become more than just a means to the satisfaction of one's needs. You can't fill up from the outside what is missing on the inside. A half-filled cup cannot overflow, while an overflowing cup nourishes many.

•Giving out of a sense of "guilt," "should," or a "savior complex" serves no one. It stunts growth and leads to obligations and resentment.

•To love means to give freely, without expecting a reciprocal return. You give of yourself completely, risking that you won't be loved in return. This is the miracle that happens each time to those who truly love: The more you give, the more love you possess for your own enjoyment. As William Shakespeare expressed it: "My bounty is as boundless as the sea, my love as deep; the more I give to thee the more I have, for both are infinite."

•When two people come together to give, then both gain, both receive. The best relationship is not 50–50 but 100–100. Each person gives 100 per cent, effortlessly, and gains a thousandfold.

EMPATHY

•An empathic concern, "Do unto others as you would have them do unto you," is another essential for a good love relationship. Each feels the other's needs as if they were his own.

•Love is having an abiding concern for the other person's relationship to themselves. The loving husband gets as much pleasure from his wife's accomplishments as his own. The pleasure and welfare of the loved one becomes as dear to us as one's self.

•Empathy is the exact opposite of self-preoccupation. The other person's feelings—pleasurable or painful—become the focus of our awareness. We do not lose our self but become more expansive.

•You give the other person the distinct feeling that you know what it is like to be in their shoes. This is tremendously reassuring and breaks down barriers of isolation and alienation. Accurate and developed empathy naturally leads to being able to put the feelings and desires of others first.

•Through sickness and health, through good times and bad, the joy of sharing allows for the pleasures to be doubled and the difficulties halved. It is a psychiatric truism that a healthy couple can bear serious illness in either partner, with concern and compassion, even using the stress as a spur to greater closeness, while a weak partnership buckles or falls apart under the strain.

ACCEPTANCE

•Love neither condemns nor condones, but seeks to accept and understand. Thoughts don't have to be screened, nor words measured. Ease and comfort prevail; you are accepted as you are.

•Minor shortcomings or endearing weaknesses add humor to affection. Perfection is not necessary. Acknowledge your inadequacies and fears as well as your hopes and desires.

•Love allows room for disagreements and conflict, pain and sadness. Love allows . . .

•An Arabian proverb describes a loving friend as one to whom you may pour out all the contents of your heart, chaff and grain together, knowing that the gentlest of hands will take and sift it, keep what is worth keeping and with a breath of kindness blow the rest away.

•It is very moving to let someone see their beauty and goodness, as if for the first time, through the acceptance you radiate from your eyes and heart.

RESPECT

•Respect is essential to love. In a healthy relationship you take joy in the other's growth and have an essential respect for their individuality.

•Webster's dictionary defines respect as noticing with attention. The loved one is not taken for granted, but seen freshly as if anew. Respect connotes more than just holding someone in high esteem, but giving to them of your time and energy.

•Lovers take pleasure in the accomplishments of the other. A wife's fame can outshine her husband's (or vice versa); there is no need for envy. Worth is based on human qualities; there is no sense of threat but rather pride.

•In a neurotic relationship there is a need to put down the other, in an attempt to build up oneself. Healthy love has no top dog or bottom dog, just two playful puppies. The other person is loved as they are, never manipulated "for their own good."

•Disdain for another may be a sign of felt weakness within oneself. A person who knows and has grown comfortable with himself, becomes more tolerant of his partner's idiosyncrasies and weaknesses. Indeed, pet foibles can make the other even more dear.

OPENNESS

•Openness means being willing to communicate your deepest feelings. Sharing ideas, values, or convictions is relatively easy. For intimacy to grow, it is feelings, both positive and negative, that must be shared.

•Openness helps overcome separateness and teaches the universality of human experience. Don't try to mystify your friends and loved ones; life on a pedestal can be mighty lonesome.

•You don't have to blab about past negativity in order to be "open," nor indiscriminately vent rage and aggression. Openness means being open to experiencing ourselves and others freshly, in a non-programmed fashion.

•Transparency, letting the energy and love from deep down shine through our emotions and intellect for others to see, is a true sharing of self. Transparency is not accomplished instantaneously but a step at a time, like peeling layers.

•Self-exposure requires some risk of being hurt; courage may be called for. But in an atmosphere of acceptance we can gradually bare the most sensitive areas of our soul. Our self-acceptance grows to incorporate our raging child, lusty sexuality, and lunatic fringe—elements which lie latent within us all. As defenses melt away, self-esteem increases; our whole world becomes more energized and lively.

HONESTY

- The growth of intimacy requires complete honesty of self-expression. Being profoundly understood and accepted is one of the great joys of love, but a precondition is you must reveal yourself. Trust in a relationship is built by being true to your deepest feelings.

- A common dread felt by most of us to varying degrees is to let anyone see through our social masks. As a result we try to impress, suppress, guard, or conceal in order not to be found out, not to stand naked before another.

- During courtship both people are image-conscious, striving to be on their best behavior. As love matures there is no need to contrive; roles and defenses can be dropped. Not that you get sloppy or inconsiderate, but it is freeing to learn that you don't have to be a mystery man or a glamour lady, that you can let your hair down and still be loved.

- Love negates fear and suspicion. Honesty means risking having your weaknesses or imperfections seen by your partner. You don't have to hide your mastectomy scar, false teeth, or psychological foibles.

- A healthy love relationship allows two people to fully know each other and—miracle of miracles—still love each other! The dropping of the guard is usually accomplished in stages over time.

PSEUDO-LOVE

•A show of love that is insincere brings shame to life. Many parents demand that their child love them simply because they have taken care of him: "Look at all we've done for you." Such guilt-instilling may lead to the pretenses of love but spill over into hostilities which grow with adolescence and adulthood.

•"Kiss your Aunt May and tell her how much you love her," is teaching a child to distort his feelings. If done with force or to excess, such distortion is the breeding ground for neurosis and sociopathy. A child is not capable of giving in love the way a fully developed adult is; it is only with the growth out of childhood that the world of "others" really starts to come into focus.

•Some may profess love while they—consciously or unconsciously—marry for different reasons: status, material security, to avoid loneliness, or to be saved from themselves.

•But pretense need not be so evident. Lust can easily be mistaken for love, not just on a physical level but on a psychological level as well. A seemingly ardent suitor may be playing out a need to subjugate, to dominate, to win a game of control with the other. He may show passion and attention during the chase, but once his "game" is snared and the trophy won, he quickly loses interest.

•Another masquerade for love, especially among the young, is the ecstatic relief felt when rebounding from a depressing home situation. Such a rebound may give rise to a hasty and ill-fated marriage, jumping from the proverbial frying pan into the fire.

•One may choose "love" to avoid the need to assert one's power or personality, or one's independence. Such a move may provide momentary relief, but growing pains will return with a fury, and to complicate the relationship as well.

•Dependency is frequently mistaken for love. Those who are lonely and afraid may latch onto someone for emotional sustenance. The high tensions of modern life lead many to seek relief in quickly manufactured "love" relationships for some feeling of self-importance and care.

•Overprotectiveness, overindulgence, and smothering are confused with love, but more often are indicative of veiled hostility. The recipient, instead of feeling free and cared for, feels claustrophobic, dependent, or manipulated—yet feels guilty because he is getting "so much love."

•Genuine love cannot oppress, inhibit, spoil, or damage. True love is balanced and respectful; it can only affirm and make whole.

LOVE IS INNOCENT

- It is not helpful to tell people that they "should" love (one cannot love because one "should" love). Love cannot be demanded by fear or pressure; this just leads to hypocrisy, contrivance, and mood-making.

- Attempts to manufacture a loving mood put a strain on the personality and inevitably backfire. No matter how hard an unhappy person tries to love, his efforts are destined for frustration because he lacks an inner sense of well-being. Better for the person to put attention on growing in his inner contentment, for out of this fullness the ability to love can grow spontaneously and effortlessly.

- Some people seek to bargain with their love: "I'll love you to the degree that you don't threaten me and help me fulfill my desires." If you love another just because he or she meets your needs, you are treating the other person as an object to be manipulated.

- Love demanded is no love at all. We cannot trick anyone into loving us. But to the degree we give it freely, love comes back to us many times over.

- Love is healthiest when it is no longer motivated by the needs for safety, control, status, or self-respect. Love is innocent; it comes of its own accord.

UNCONDITIONAL LOVE

•Each of us is unique and of unconditional value—this is our birthright.

•Am I loved for myself? Or is it because I am
—Good
—Admirable
—Pretty
—Strong
—Helpless
—Sick

•Love at its height is unconditional. It is given without thought, whether or not the loved one will reciprocate. There are no "ifs" or "buts," no strings attached. Love is given freely.

•Love can say "no" when discipline or firmness is needed, but does so in a "yes" fashion conveying security and acceptance.

•The person is loved as he is, not for what he once was or is expected to be. In a love relationship each person seeks to promote the uniqueness and individuality of the other, according to his own standards and inner vision.

•To develop this higher love is not easy. It is a lofty achievement to be able to radiate love without any thought of return, and with a full willingness to grant total freedom to the beloved.

•Realistically, only the saints among us are capable of giving unconditional love all of the time. Most of us have our capacity to love limited to some degree by our needs, expectations, and emotional scars. But let us have unconditional love as our ideal. Though the human condition is imperfect, let us love our condition unconditionally.

LIVING LOVE

•Life is progressive. Lend yourself to its flow and it will carry you to higher and higher levels of love and integration, to a spontaneous here-and-now appreciation of all of life's blessings.

•Living love is seeing yourself and all of nature in everyone, and everyone and all of nature in yourself.

•Life becomes one miraculous happening after another.

•You have more than you need. There is less fear, insecurity, or vulnerability. The separation and conflict disappear; love permeates all aspects of your life.

THE PATH TO LOVE

- Just as there is a natural path for the acorn's becoming a mighty oak tree and for the caterpillar's becoming a beautiful butterfly, so too, there are necessary stages in the development of your full potential for love and happiness.

- It is not a matter of trying harder; the acorn doesn't have to try to become an oak tree.

- It is not a matter of waiting for the right person to love (as we shall discover in our next section).

- It is a matter of recognizing how the growth and development of love unfolds, and then lending yourself to that process.

- It is a matter of
  GROWING
  SHARING
  TRANSCENDING

GROWING

—A Loving Birthright
—Well Begun Is Half Done
—Adolescent Love
—Growing Pains
—Emotional Blocks to the Flow of Love
—Overcoming Guilt
—Love Thy Self
—A Self-love Checklist
—Pretense/Defense
—Love's Great Dampener: Chronic Fatigue
—The Mask of Depression
—Up from Depression
—Your Self-image
—Self-inventory
—Mirror, Mirror, on the Wall
—Self-esteem Building
—Health Is Your Opportunity
—The "Sweet" Life
—Fitness Can Be Fun
—Stretching Exercises
—Develop Your Person Power
—Assertive Training
—Afraid to Love?
—Don Juan Syndrome
—The Practice of Love
—What We Put Attention on Grows Stronger
—The Expansion of Happiness
—R_x for Dis-ease
—A Calm Mind
—The Healing Silence
—When the Need for Psychotherapy?
—The Therapeutic Process
—Guidelines for Change
—Self-mastery
—Cultivate Preferences
—Finding Your Dharma
—Love's Labor
—Search for Excellence
—Success
—Love Blossoms in the Soil of Happiness
—Refined Appreciation
—Attractiveness
—The Right Model
—Self-actualization
—The Loving Person
—The World Is as You Are
—Birds of a Feather Flock Together

A LOVING BIRTHRIGHT

•The belief that we humans are born evil, selfish, or "animalistic" and that we need to be conditioned or controlled into becoming good and loving persons is still a predominant mode of thought. This represents a grave misunderstanding of the doctrine of "original sin" and, more recently, of psychoanalytic theory.

•The infant is more than a "fallen creature," more than a "caldron of seething excitations." Helpless and needy, yes, but bad, no.

•Three decades of infant and child development research have shown, to put it simply, that human beings are born good. " 'Good' in the sense that there is no evil or hostility in them," explains noted scientist Ashley Montagu, "but that at birth they are wholly prepared, equipped, to function as creatures who not only want and need to be loved by others but who also want and need to love others."*

•From birth, we are highly intelligent beings programmed for fulfillment and the expansion of love. The potential is there, but just like the giant redwood growing from a seed to a mighty monument of nature, environmental conditions must be proper.

* Ashley Montagu, *The Direction of Human Development,* rev. ed. Hawthorn Books, Inc., New York, 1970, page 289.

WELL BEGUN IS HALF DONE

•The most essential requirement for our growth and development—aside from survival needs of air, food, water, and shelter—is love. The experience of love during the first five years is the source of virtually all our well-being and happiness.

•Motherly love instills the most essential blessing of all—love for life.

•Mother provides our first intimate, social, and sensuous experience; the pattern and matrix for all future love relationships. "She who rocks the cradle, rules the world"—especially our psychological world.

•Our picture of the world—whether it is safe or troubled, loving or insecure—is mostly internalized through our interactions with Mother.

•Childhood experience forms the building blocks of love: Safety, trust, control and letting go, dependency and autonomy. If we have the good fortune of being properly loved, we are halfway home.

ADOLESCENT LOVE

•The teens are a time when temporary crushes and infatuations spring up. Ah yes, who can forget the innocence, excitement—and clumsiness—of first love?

•With the onrush of sexual energies and impending adulthood, the adolescent may be burdened with self-doubt and uncertainty. He may need to impress his peers with his masculinity and prowess. Just as medieval knights sought to win their lady's hand in tournament battles, so the modern youth may take to the football field to gain acceptance from some dreamed-of cheerleader.

•Rejection of his family ties is not uncommon during an adolescent's tumultuous drive for independence. What a time this can be for teen-agers and parents alike!

•Keep in mind that a modicum of rebelliousness may presage a healthy adulthood; it is the emergence of individuality. Most adults who wind up in a psychiatrist's office have never really had an adolescence. The instinctual forces of adolescence, sexual and aggressive, must be integrated into the adult personality.

GROWING PAINS

•With each stage of life there is gain but also loss. We leave childhood dreams, school, jobs, loved ones, and our youth behind. So it is with nature: The rose blooms as the seed is lost, winter's end is spring's beginning. Each loss sets the stage for further creation.

•Pain is not necessarily a bad thing. If there has been a loss, it is a sign that healing is already under way. Be with the pain, get the support and comforting you need, for it will take time to heal.

•Pain also signals us to learn, to see what law of nature we've been violating, to change, get on to a higher course of action.

•Do not feel threatened by growth. You may take a faltering step forward and stumble, but this is the road to mastery. The only real mistake is a failure to learn from your experiences.

•Don't be afraid to be human–to be yourself. With each growth step, we separate from something that was, and become more and more a unique individual.

•Being yourself isn't always easy. During rough times you may be tempted to give up your ideals and lose yourself to conformity. Have faith in your inner voice. Don't seek to live someone else's life; it's just not you. You have something really valuable to contribute to the world, but only through the expression of your own personality.

•"If a man does not keep pace with his companions," suggested Henry David Thoreau, "perhaps it is because he hears the beat of a different drummer. Let him step to the music he hears, however measured or far away."

EMOTIONAL BLOCKS TO THE FLOW OF LOVE

•A human being free of fear and emotionally secure can best satisfy others. If fears and insecurities remain, to whatever degree, damage to our full humanity may result. These are the "little scars" we all carry around inside us which cause unnecessary suffering to ourselves and others.

•Emotional wounds that do not heal properly entangle our love life in pain, conflict, and inhibitions. No matter how careful we are, we seem to hurt the ones we love and limit our satisfactions.

•Snobbery, temper tantrums, ridicule, poor self-image, worry, and bearing grudges sap our vital life energy. Our energy is locked in or spent wastefully, instead of creating waves of fulfillment and joy.

•Nature is forever kind to us. Even if we've had inadequate mothering or painful life experiences, most emotional damage is potentially reversible.

•Love, happiness, and serenity are awaiting you. All we need do, as we shall be learning, is lend nature a hand with eliminating the blocks.

•Becoming a full person is the key—taking responsibility for your own growth and maturation.

OVERCOMING GUILT

•Too many people still believe that they are innately sinful or evil; that the nature of life is to suffer. Unnecessary guilt may be the result of parental rage being vented upon us as children, or frequently being told how "bad" we are.

•In its most severe forms the person has a deeply imbedded self-hatred which leads him unconsciously to seek out punishment. He may confess to a crime he did not commit or hurt himself physically. The guilt-ridden may seek out brutal or destructive mates to recreate the harsh parenting of childhood.

•The self-destructive habits of alcoholics may be acting out an unconscious cycle of guilt-punishment-more guilt. Alcoholics Anonymous and Alanon, for the alcoholic and his family, can help to break this habit.

•More commonly, people suffer from an endless array of mini-guilts, punishing themselves with self-inflicted "buzzes" of anxiety. Mini-guilts are often the result of internalized "shoulds" and "shouldn'ts." Learn to substitute a softer, more understanding, "It would be nice if . . ." for your punishing "shoulds." Try it, keep practicing; nature is on your side.

•There has never been a person on this earth who has not done "something" he later regretted. Acceptance and forgiveness begin at home. We're not perfect, that's why we're here.

•Life is meant to grow in satisfaction. The Talmud holds a man responsible for any pleasure in life he has passed by. C'mon, be nice to yourself. Give yourself permission, enjoy!

LOVE THY SELF

•To love oneself is not a sin—to the contrary, not to give ourselves the same modicum of love and respect that every human being deserves is a sin. To thine own self be attentive, patient, and kind.

•Avoid straining—most of us have been taught that we have to try to become more loving, try harder in order to deserve more love. Don't push yourself, complain about yourself, or denounce yourself—you're beautiful just the way you are.

•Love of self is the opposite of selfishness. The selfish person lacks self-love and so stays chronically needy. This endless "shopping list" of needs, demands, and expectations fails to bring him lasting satisfaction. The cure for selfishness is more love, especially from within.

•Intimacy with self teaches us the commonality of all human experience. The great irony, the great paradox is that the deeper inside yourself you go, the more in touch with yourself you are, the closer you are to others. Love of self—nurturing of oneself—is the basis for understanding and appreciating others.

A SELF-LOVE CHECKLIST

- Self-love is not self-indulgence, poor impulse control, or blaming others.

- Self-love is
  - —giving yourself approval.
  - —talking to yourself gently, with affection.
  - —trusting your inner voice and intuition.
  - —a commitment to developing your full potential and creativity.
  - —understanding all your actions; giving yourself the benefit of the doubt.
  - —self-forgiveness; getting over that guilty feeling.
  - —having fun, lots of it; being free and easy.
  - —taking responsibility for yourself; developing your own values, rules, and regulations.
  - —treating yourself to a great vacation, a hot bubble bath, or your favorite piece of music.
  - —knowing when to say "yes," and when to say "no."
  - —taking risks for your own advancement.
  - —letting yourself enjoy winning or losing, wealth, or an average income.
  - —affirming yourself, letting yourself succeed.
  - —feeling pleasure fully; knowing you deserve it.
  - —loving your body, from fitness to your sexuality.
  - —"yes," giving yourself permission.
  - —providing yourself with life-supporting and enriching people, food, and ideas.
  - —surrounding yourself with beauty, especially the natural.
  - —taking in the affection and compliments of others, allowing others to be your friends.

PRETENSE/DEFENSE

•To the extent that we have stress, guilt, and shame in our mental storehouse, we tend to hide behind our social roles and masks. The true self is felt to be weak, ugly, or afraid and so a wall of "defense mechanisms" is constructed. Such a psychic life may be safe, but it is also lonely, for love is kept locked within.

•We lose our authenticity and become—less feeling, more superficial—performers. Contempt, cockiness, belligerence, and hypercriticism are often a camouflage for a wounded soul. The need for love is repressed; to replace it we may instead seek out admiration or sexual conquests.

•But social masks are worn only as long as they are needed. A wounded soul, as will be discussed, can heal.

•Do not try to rip off the mask of another. Brutal confrontation may momentarily weaken someone's defenses, but will very soon make him/her hold on that much tighter. Indifference to pretense, and acceptance of the person's real self, allows the barriers to be shed in a gradual manner.

LOVE'S GREAT DAMPENER: CHRONIC FATIGUE

•To feel fresh and vibrant is necessary to the growth of love and happiness.

•Chronic fatigue is the complaint heard most in doctors' offices.

•The signs and symptoms of chronic fatigue are:

—Dullness
—Pouches under the eyes
—Poor muscle tone
—Pasty, pale complexion
—Lack of spontaneity of gesture
—Greater tendency to be bored or depressed
—More fear, tension, and anxiety
—Decreased cooperativeness
—Less acceptance of constructive criticism
—Increased irritability, temper outbursts
—Lowered attention span
—Impaired recent memory
—Decreased libido (sex drive)
—Insomnia, waking up tired
—Vague, generalized, somatic complaints
—Decreased interest in personal care
—Drug and alcohol abuse
—Lowered baseline satisfaction

Is it any wonder that chronic fatigue is such an inhibitor of love and well-being?

•Causes of chronic fatigue:

—In our society, too little rather than too much physical activity is more frequently a cause.

—Time-pressure demands
—Stimulus overload
—Insufficient sleep
—Biorhythm disturbances, e.g., jet lag
—Family, medical, and social problems
—Monotonous or tedious work
—Not enough quiet-time or time alone
—Frequent false alarms, as in anxiety neurosis
—Preconscious psychological conflicts
—Loss of a love
—Low-grade depression

THE MASK OF DEPRESSION

•All too often depression is misdiagnosed or overlooked. Fifteen million Americans suffer a medically significant depression each year; of these only one and one-half million receive therapy. These statistics on serious depression say nothing of the minor depressions that on occasion trouble almost everyone.

•It is sometimes very hard to recognize when we or someone close to us is depressed. All depressions are not the same; they vary considerably in duration and degree. While its symptoms may vary, depression always impairs the ability to enjoy everyday living.

•Signs and symptoms that will help you to recognize a low-grade to moderate depression in you or someone who is close to you, are as follows:

- –A pessimistic, critical attitude. Everyone (from your spouse to coworkers at the office) and everything (from the stock-market to the weather) seem to contribute to your feeling gloomy and uncomfortable.
- –Marked irritability. You may tend to get upset at the most trivial matters, such as a waiter who is slow to serve you or difficulty with finding a parking space. You have more temper outbursts or difficulty saying anything positive.
- –Difficulty in making decisions. You may suffer gnawing doubts about choice of job, spouse, place to live, and career path. Or the most trivial matters may cause trouble: what to wear or where to go for dinner.
- –Loss of interest. A special project, hobby, friends, or food no longer bring you pleasure. Your energy is low, you seem to lack motivation.

—Difficulty in concentrating. You may have difficulty adding a column of figures or recalling a magazine article you just read.
—Inability to laugh. Unprovoked crying spells or feelings of guilt may plague you. Your muscles may ache; you may feel listless or exhausted.
—Decrease in sexual vitality. You may not be interested in making love as often as usual, or you may experience a temporary bout of impotence or difficulty with having an orgasm. In some cases, promiscuity or a sudden affair may signal an inner struggle with depression.
—Difficulty with sleep. Especially if you are persistently suffering from early-morning insomnia, your depression may be getting worse.

•A depression can be lurking behind a variety of masks. Common means of attempting to hide a depression are compulsive eating, excessive drinking, overworking, adultery, compulsive gambling, drug abuse, and a wide array of physical disorders.

•Survey what's been going on in your life. Loss may frequently precipitate a depression. A common denominator in most depression is the loss of someone or something highly valued:
—the death of a spouse
—divorce, separation, the breakup of a love relationship
—a serious illness or injury
—a failure at school or work
—a major financial loss
—moving
—success (the loss of striving)
—midlife loss of "youth," "beauty," or opportunity
—failure or frustration of a cherished ideal or goal
—retirement

•Fatigue, poor self-esteem, hereditary predisposition, or a quick series of disappointments can predispose to depression. Depression is very human and common to us all.

•Acute depressions are generally self-limiting. The longer a depression has been developing, the longer it may take to see improvement. A serious depression may require psychiatric support. Know that recovery from depression may not be a smooth process but full of ups and downs, dramatic leaps and painful backslides.

• The question of suicide—is best kept a question. The awful, black feeling will pass. If you fear that you may act on suicidal thoughts or are losing control, help is available twenty-four hours a day through hospital emergency rooms.

• A major emotional loss can trigger a prolonged grief reaction. Full recovery from a major loss, such as the death of a spouse or loved one, may take one year or longer before the individual can truly come to a point of understanding and acceptance.

• It's O.K. to feel angry. Anger always accompanies a major loss. Don't take it out on yourself. Beat a pillow, kick a bed, yell, scream (a car parked in a deserted place makes a great scream-chamber), or hit a punching bag. Get the anger out in these harmless, helpful ways. You'll avoid senseless arguments, accidents, and ulcers.

• The most common variety is a low-grade depression. Such depression is usually the result of chronic stress and anxiety, which sap the body's energy and vital resources. As fatigue accumulates, life becomes "a drag"; the individual loses motivation.

• Non-prescribed drugs have become a primary means by which people attempt to cope with emotional letdowns. Alcohol may provide a temporary lift, but deepens a depression and may precipitate violent outbursts. Food can provide temporary excitement and security; compulsive overeating may be a misplaced attempt to cope with an underlying depression.

• When coping with a loss, get lots of rest, stick to your routine, and keep decision-making to a minimum. It also helps to anticipate a positive outcome, pamper yourself, get some of your mother's chicken soup, seek out close friends, and buy yourself a new wardrobe, fresh plants, or a kitten.†

† See Melba Colgrove, Harold H. Bloomfield, and Peter McWilliams, *How to Survive the Loss of a Love.* Simon & Schuster, New York, 1976.

YOUR SELF-IMAGE

•To love means to give of oneself; to give of oneself, one must first value oneself. Self-image lies at the root of most of our social interactions. Almost all psychological problems, from neurosis to paranoia, and from hysteria to criminality, stem from a lack of self-worth.

•The healthy person has the baseline feeling, "I love being me." This is not vanity, selfishness, or a hyperinflated ego; it is self-celebration. True love of others is based on love of self.

•You have the right to expect others to treat you with dignity and respect, but you must first begin by treating yourself that way. Stop telling yourself that you are stupid, inferior, ugly, inadequate, or crazy. If you are saying that to yourself, you're communicating these messages to others (through posture, tone of voice, facial expression, words, or body language).

•Self-image gets reflected back to us. It may seem as though others or "the world" are doing this damage to you, while in actuality, you are doing it to yourself. Poor self-image sets you up for rejection, criticism, and negativity from others. For better and for worse we often get what we feel we deserve.

SELF-INVENTORY

•It's time to take stock of your most precious commodity—yourself—before you move on to building an even more powerful and loving you.

•How do you feel about yourself? Choose ten adjectives which describe the real you, then amplify. What are the things you most dislike about yourself? What about yourself do you most try to conceal from others? What is the greatest obstacle to your self-acceptance? Are you embarrassed by liking yourself? What are your most admirable and endearing qualities?

•What experiences in your life were the most humiliating? Which the most fear-inducing? In an intimate conversation, how comfortable are you expressing anger, fear, felt weaknesses, or love? Where do stress or tension manifest in your body; are you engaged in any program to get rid of them?

•Look at yourself through the eyes of your friends as well as strangers; what impressions do you make on others? How well does this correspond with who you really are? Are you comfortable needing others or do you find it difficult to ask for and accept help? If you died, what would people say about you?

•Are you able to discuss your deepest problems and concerns with another? How do you feel about emotional commitment? Are you fearful of being rejected or trapped? What has been the pattern of your love relationships—in childhood, adolescence, and adult life?

•A personal journal is a useful tool. Use a free-flowing style so there is less chance of censorship. Journal time is a good time for personal reflection, to express your deepest self. Over time, it will be fascinating for you to see the flow and changing pattern of your life.

MIRROR, MIRROR ON THE WALL

•How you feel about your body is crucial to your self-esteem. So many of us are afflicted with a poor body image, especially genital shame: "I'm too fat," "I'm too skinny," "My body is awkward and ugly," "My penis is too small," "My breasts are saggy," "I have stretch marks . . . scars . . . warts . . ."

•A good exercise is to stand nude in front of a full-length mirror. How do you feel about your body? What parts of your body do you like best? Which arouse a sense of shame or weakness? Are you comfortable with your sexuality? What kinds of clothes do you wear? What are you trying to cover, what are you trying to show?

•Now look into the mirror and tell yourself "I love you." Say it several times out loud. At first you may feel strange, embarrassed, or foolish—but do it. Say again "I love you" and your name. Take you time. Love away in each bodily area the felt weakness and shame. Keep loving yourself out loud until you see yourself with a relaxed, happy expression. Bravo!

•Almost all forms of nudity are body-liberating experiences. When you confront your body visually, you can begin to change. Continually find things about your body that you like; never mind the flaws. Praise yourself: Try giving yourself a total body massage.

•Observe your posture; learn how to stand more straight. To overcome your "slump" will require thought, practice, and feedback from your friends. Daily yoga exercises, martial arts, or

Rolfing may also be of help. Walking around erect—back straight, chin up, shoulders back, pelvis tucked under, genitals forward—will significantly change how you relate to yourself and the world.

•Loosen up your body. Stretch and bend your spine and joints. Breathe deeply and fully; when you exhale, let go. Dance in front of a mirror, by yourself or with friends. Move your pelvis, shoulders, neck, and legs. Be outrageous; let it all hang out. Shake, rattle, and roll!

SELF-ESTEEM BUILDING

•The social feedback loop can work for you as well as against you. The more you uncritically and lovingly accept yourself, the more others will be free to love and appreciate you.

•Tell yourself a few times a day, especially any time you are getting down on yourself, that though you may be working on some "growth edges," at your core you are a good, intelligent, loving human being.

•Negative childhood self-esteem inputs can be erased using affirmations. Affirmations are positive thoughts that you consciously choose to implant within your consciousness to produce a desirable result. For example, repeat to yourself out loud the affirmation, "I like myself; I approve of myself; I am a lovable person."

•While you are engaged in this self-talk, monitor your voice, facial expressions, and body language. Make sure especially then, and throughout the day, that you look and feel like the beautiful being that you are: head high, shoulders back, chest up, voice firm and with expression.

•Just as we can weight-lift to build up the muscles in our bodies, we can use these affirmations to build up a weakened ego. It is essential to practice regularly and to catch yourself early in any process of downgrading yourself. With repetition of an affirmation for a month or two, your negative thought forms will fall away.

HEALTH IS YOUR OPPORTUNITY

- Self-image also depends on our body—how it feels and how we feel about it. Dullness and inertia of the body inhibit free emotional flow, love-making, and over-all mental functioning.

- If you are walking around with slumped shoulders, stiff joints, a colorless, wrinkled complexion, weakness, or a lack of vitality, you are constricting your capacity for love and joy. Getting fit will not only help you to avoid illness and premature aging, but, more important, to feel optimally good.‡

- Your habits of daily living are crucial determinants of your health. A routine of no smoking, moderate drinking, seven or eight hours sleep per night, regular meals with no between-meal snacking, breakfast every day, normal weight, and moderate regular exercise can increase your life expectancy by more than ten years. You will not only live longer, but be a real dynamo of energy.

- Health is primarily your responsibility. Your doctor or a competent holistic health center can help you to design a program to lose weight, stop smoking, decrease your alcohol intake, or get into shape, but your participation—actively—is the vital ingredient. Change will come slowly, and your enthusiasm may at times plateau, but stick to your holistic health program and benefits will systematically accrue.

‡ Harold H. Bloomfield and Robert Kory, *The Holistic Way to Health and Happiness.* Simon & Schuster, New York, 1978.

- Keep in mind that the longer you have undermined your health through chronic stress, emotional tension, and poor health habits, the longer it may take you to notice significant progress toward greater wellness. Use will power but don't strain. Focus on enjoying each step of the way.

THE "SWEET" LIFE

•The average American consumes more than a hundred pounds of refined sugar annually. But sugar is meant to be used as a condiment, not a food. We are a nation of sugarholics.

•After a brief energy boost, sugar drains your long-term energy and vitality. A good slug of sugar—a candy bar, pie à la mode, or chewing gum—will make you nervous, lethargic, and ravenously hungry. Because it provides lots of calories, empty of proteins, vitamins, or bulk, sugar is the chief culprit in obesity.

•Not only does excessive sugar consumption contribute to about half the U.S. population being overweight, it also leads down the path to degenerative disease, especially diabetes, tooth decay, and hypoglycemia. Also, a diet of sugar-heavy processed, man-made or quick-snack foods robs you of the nutritional content and vitality of real organic food.

•In addition to the obvious sugar intake through cakes, pies, pastries, soft drinks, and sugar added to coffee or tea, we engorge our bodies with sugar in unseen ways. Read the food labels next time you shop. You'll find large amounts of sugar in soups, baked beans, ketchup, Jell-O, salad dressing, cereal, and hundreds of other products you eat.

•Cut down on your sugar consumption. You don't have to be a fanatic—an infrequent favorite dessert may be fine. However, you ought to discover the joys of natural, wholesome foods. Substitute them for sugary processed foods whenever possible.

FITNESS CAN BE FUN

•Regular exercise is very important to your health and happiness. An exercise routine contributes to a radiant appearance, an erect posture, and a positive mental attitude, in addition to cultivating your optimal well-being. It also helps curb your appetite and keep your weight down.

•Nature designed your body for the enjoyment of physical activity. You were meant to run, swim, walk, climb, or engage in sports. Exercise does not have to be boring or exhausting but can be fun. Choose a fitness program you enjoy, build up slowly; the exhilaration is sure to come.

•Hundreds of thousands of previously sedentary people are getting back into shape and loving it. They clear the exercise hurdle and report increased energy, reduced fatigue, improved resistance to disease, greater self-esteem, and enhanced sexual vitality.

•You don't have to make major changes in your life style to become fit. There are three principal components to a fit and active life style:

- —Endurance. Fifteen to twenty minutes four to five times weekly do some aerobic exercise (jogging, swimming, tennis, bicycling) that gets your heart and circulatory system going. The idea is to breathe hard but still be able to carry on a conversation.
- —Coordination and Strength. The objective is not muscle beach, but a muscle system that serves you.
- —Flexibility. Stretch, shake, and move your body more.

STRETCHING EXERCISES

•For maximum joy and vitality we need to keep our body flexible and elastic. More stretching, twisting, reaching, and bending must be incorporated into our daily routine. Flexibility is part of fitness, and fun.

•When you wake up in the morning consider enjoying a good stretch, first in bed and then standing up. Reach for the sky on your tiptoes, then bend over and let your arms dangle. Without straining, try to touch your toes. To get your circulation going run in place, do a few jumping jacks, or shake yourself about.

•Take opportunities to stretch and bend throughout the day. Try some of these exercises right now. Put the book down and stretch your neck by slowly rolling your head in a complete circle three times to the left, then three times to the right. Massage your neck where it is particularly stiff to help the letting go.

•You can give your torso a good stretch by sitting forward in your chair and twisting as far as you can in both directions to look behind you. Move your arms up, back, and around in a circular motion a few times. Hyperextend your head and back, then bring your head forward and let it dangle between your knees.

•A lot of us hold tension in our lower back. Lie on your back on the floor, then bring both knees to your chest. With your hands upon your knees, as is comfortable, gently roll from side to side.

•Consider taking yoga or dance classes. If you already have a back or musculoskeletal problem, consult with your physician.

DEVELOP YOUR PERSON POWER

•Develop and assert your person power—take full responsibility for your happiness and well-being. Power doesn't mean being hostile, overaggressive, or coercive; it means being confident, self-actualizing, and free.

•Person power does not require straining to be a superman, but is a natural consequence to holistic personality development. Get into a self-improvement habit in all areas: body, senses, emotions, intellect, skills, relationships, and spirit. Learn to enjoy your expanding potential, not feel compulsive about it.

•Balance is important. Don't develop one area of your personality at the cost of another. The concert pianist needs some tennis, the tennis pro a concert.

•Get to know yourself. Your likes, dislikes, and preferences. Alone time doesn't have to mean loneliness. Acquiesce to your whims, have fun!

•Determine your own life style. Find out where, how, and with whom you want to live. Don't go by the standards and values of others; discover what's important to you.

•Women especially need to feel more comfortable with self-determination. The more powerful a woman/person you become, the more attractive you'll be to yourself—and others—in the long run.

ASSERTIVE TRAINING

• If you feel overly meek, compliant, or passive, assertive training (AT) can help expand your emotional freedom. Fear of rejection in intimate relations, taking initiative, or standing up to others may be causing you stagnation at work, undeveloped relations, mental anguish, or physical problems ranging from migraine to impotence.

• AT would aim at increasing your ability to express real feelings in appropriate, effective ways. Assertive behaviors that might need learning range from forthright statements of indignation, annoyance, and resentment, to genuine expressions of gratitude, approval, and love.

• AT includes a high degree of specificity and meticulous attention to detail. In a warm and supportive manner, attention would be paid not only to words used, but to your whole mode of expression: tone of voice, inflection, posture, eye contact, and facial expression. You would be guided through specific behavioral rehearsals, including role-playing, before gradually transferring this "classroom work" to real-life situations.

• Assertiveness should not be confused with inappropriately venting hostile feelings, one-upmanship, or deceptive games. AT involves finding the best way to meet your needs in consonance with the needs of others and the environment.

AFRAID TO LOVE?

•Many people either avoid love or force it out of their lives. They may concentrate on work or a cause, but remain emotionally blocked off.

•Disappointment in love leaves some with their confidence shattered. A broken heart needs time to heal after a divorce or traumatic love affair. A temporary withdrawal, for even a few months, may provide a necessary reprieve.

•But for others rejection of love threatens to become a lifelong pattern. There may be an unconscious dread that someone will see through their social façade to the evil, shallowness, or inadequacy that lies lurking beneath. As a result, only superficial and distant friendships are maintained . . . a "lone wolf" he remains.

•Some repress love because that was their parental model. Theirs was a "cold fish" or "stiff upper lip" family that looked upon affection as awkward or with embarrassment. Worse yet, perhaps rage—not love—dominated their upbringing.

•Some reject love because they are too perfectionistic; always demanding too much from a person, never satisfied. An earlier love experience may have seemed so "pure," that any future love seems distasteful.

•Accepting the care of an aged mother or father, putting a brother or sister through college, or taking on major civic responsibilities—noble as these undertakings are—may represent a convenient means for avoiding intimacy.

•Loneliness is always a failure of loving as much as being loved. The more love is blocked, the more intense become the symptoms. Love is too powerful an energy to be locked in without suffering.

DON JUAN SYNDROME

• The desire to seduce women into an endless succession of transient, superficial relationships is known as the Don Juan syndrome. Don Juan was a legendary Spanish personage who was reputed to be a most charming and beguiling lover. For most men Don Juanism is a temporary phase, which is outgrown as deeper and more meaningful pleasures of intimacy set in.

• For some, Don Juanism becomes a way of life and may represent a defense against being vulnerable or weak. The compulsive seducer may have to repeatedly prove his masculinity or allay homosexual fears. Perhaps he cannot bear the threat of rejection, criticism, or being humbled.

• Love may also be blocked because of the presence of great hostility. The Don Juan doesn't risk opening himself up for fear of hurting or wishing to do away with the person for whom "love" is felt. Underneath his charm may lie a secret hatred for women.

• He may have a terrible fear of being left alone or abandoned. A list of amorous involvements provides a kind of insurance that if he loses one, she is not indispensable but quickly replaceable.

• You might play psychiatrist for a while; see how many other explanations you can come up with!

THE PRACTICE OF LOVE

•There is an art to loving, as Erich Fromm suggested. Like any art, love stems from that which is innate, but it can be cultivated and practiced. If you have been restricted in your flow of love, "exercises" can help you infuse love into your every action.

•Balanced personality development implies not only the ability to stand up for one's rights, but also a capacity for volunteering praise and approval. Systematically and comfortably, you can learn more loving habits.

•When the feeling arises, and when appropriate, begin to utter the following sorts of statements:

—Our friendship is very precious to me.
—You look really terrific in that outfit.
—I very much appreciate your kindness and generosity.
—You handled that difficult situation admirably.
—I feel good when I'm around you.
—You're beautiful.
—I love you very much.

•There is no need for a gushing sentimentality or saccharine flattery. The goal is to be able to express appreciation and positive regard, freely and appropriately. Actions too, from offering your subway seat to an older person, to helping a friend with homework, to giving a needed hug or massage to your loved one, can be systematically self-monitored and increased.

•Keep a diary and make a chart; look for specific more loving behaviors. From a nice chit-chat with the grocery clerk to bringing flowers home and making dinner, you can find creative expression for your loving talents. Practicing more loving words and actions may seem volitional and self-conscious for a while, but these will quickly become more automatic.

•Love sometimes means taking a risk, being vulnerable. Remember, though, "It *is* better to have loved and lost than never to have loved at all." More rewarding relationships will soon firmly establish you in your new and more loving ways.

WHAT WE PUT ATTENTION ON GROWS STRONGER

- If you focus exclusively on negativity—worries, problems, fears, suspicion—that will grow stronger in your life. If you favor love and goodness (not mood-make, just favor that which is already there), then these will blossom even more in your life.

- The fault-finder will find faults even in paradise. Let yourself be governed by your admirations rather than by your disgusts.

- With the right mental attitude "problems" become opportunities for growth, for exercising our talents. "What ifs" become "so what ifs" as your worries melt away.

- Appreciate the simple pleasures: For a few minutes deliberately walk and look about you in slow motion. Experience the miracles of creation that are here to be enjoyed.

- Find your love in the present, in the eternal here-and-now, not just in a sentimental past or some hoped-for future. "Awake at dawn with a winged heart and give thanks for another day of loving." (Kahlil Gibran)

THE EXPANSION OF HAPPINESS

•While human activity is dominated by a search for happiness, happiness has remained elusive for most people. One group says wealth is the key, while another says that happiness lies in a simple life with no luxuries. Does love assure happiness? Fulfillment of duty to family, country, or God has been called the path to happiness as has the return to nature, to sensual pleasures, or to simply "doing your own thing."

•Which way to turn in your search for greater happiness? Along the highway to happiness there are many dead-end streets. Here are some pointers to help you along the way.

•No amount of striving is going to win you lasting happiness. No amount of manipulating other people and situations in your life is going to lead to fulfillment. If we cannot find contentment in ourselves, it is useless to seek it elsewhere.

•The quest for ever greater stimulation and excitement breeds only short-term happiness. Excitement is a state of hyperarousal that has to physiologically rebound. As a result, excitement addicts inevitably must experience periods of boredom, frustration, and depression. A frantic search for "What's next?" soon becomes a despairing "Why bother?"

•Happiness does not come by trying or making a mood. Nor does it come by avoiding things that are unpleasant, such as admitting a mistake or sticking by your spouse during a long illness.

•So what is the key to happiness, to a life of fulfillment? It is twofold: Grow to your full potential, raise your level of consciousness, by developing a maximum of ease, order, and contentment within and by having your sights and activities geared to serving a larger cause, a more universal end.

•A stable, fully integrated nervous system is the basis for achieving 200 per cent fulfillment, 100 per cent inner and 100 per cent outer. Happiness expands through inward and outward strokes. We find rich inner resources of love and happiness and bring these out through progressive actions.

•There is an old saying, "Happiness is like a kiss—to get any good out of it you have to give it to someone else!" Happiness is a by-product of being useful to others or devoted to a worthy cause.

•Aiming high, letting the highest principles guide your life, we find happiness by the way. Fixing our minds upon one's own little personal joys and gratifications yields only transitory pleasures. Orienting our lives to the well-being of others, some art form, or the improvement of mankind, gives our enjoyment the status of eternity.

•As our happiness expands we learn a noble truth: The highest form of pleasure comes to the person who gives himself in love.

R_X FOR DIS-EASE

• Stress is a contagious dis-ease. Every time you react with anger, fear, or resentment you trigger negativity and defensiveness in others. There is enough negativity in the world without contributing to it further.

• Whenever possible, avoid making important decisions or taking action when you are emotionally upset. Your action will be more effective if you wait until you are serene and centered.

• It always takes two to have an argument. One person staying calm can soothe another's hurt or angry heart. Hostility and emotional uptightness do not have to be met with resentment or irritation.

• Eliminate your "red buttons"—automatic responses of fear, anger, or jealousy—gain increasing degrees of freedom and serenity. As you learn to feel more ease where you once felt uptight, to accept with greater equanimity that which has been irritating you, your red buttons will become pink buttons and eventually disappear.

• This does not mean you become a "pushover," a "wallflower," or don't respond to criticism. On the contrary, you become more dynamic, more creative, in taking whatever assertive action is necessary. Staying calm and centered enhances your capacity to choose a proper course of action.

• The internal fires don't have to be raging to firmly but calmly inform someone that, "It angers me when you . . . ," followed by a constructive input. As the ancient Bhagavad Gita teaches, establish yourself in inner tranquility as the basis for effective action.

A CALM MIND

•A calm mind is the foundation for happiness. It enables you to witness the full panorama of life's joys; to turn obstacles into opportunities, problems into achievements. The natural tendency of the mind is to seek out a field of greater happiness. A calm mind naturally grows in contentment.

•The person who lacks inner contentment is at the mercy of his environment for his sense of well-being. For one with inner stability, living becomes not just coping but a delightful growth process. Strong thought producing effective action, in the face of life's pressures, generates fulfillment and heightened self-esteem.

•"If you would make a man happy," teaches Seneca, "do not add to his possessions but subtract from the sum of his desires." We grow in serenity as we become free of vain desires, wild expectations, and worrisome fears.

•Except for life-threatening situations we are safer without fear! A clear mind allows us to perceive and accurately react to our environment. Fear makes us tense and cuts down enjoyment tremendously.

•It is tragic to believe that tension is necessary for creativity and motivation. Pressure of time and circumstances can sometimes produce much finer work but only from a mind which is free and relaxed, which does not become tense under pressure.

•A gentle and unflappable temper is a boon to its owner and all who surround him. A tranquil mind shines forth acceptance and appreciation for all.

THE HEALING SILENCE

•Too many individuals in our "Future Shock" western culture are suffering from too much emergency (fight-flight) response too much of the time. This accumulated stress contributes to dis-ease, dis-order, and dis-satisfaction.

•We need a mental exercise to master stress and develop our full human potential. The regular experience of the healing silence* rejuvenates body, mind, and spirit. But how? There are many techniques, with varying degrees of effectiveness, from which to choose. You must decide which is right for you.

•The easiest way to begin including more silence in your life is to close your eyes and relax for ten minutes or more once to twice a day. Winston Churchill and Harry Truman were but two of many world leaders who used brief rest periods of this sort to renew their energy and vitality. All you will need is a room where you won't be disturbed and a comfortable couch or chair.

•Positive imagery can be used to create a relaxed mood. Sit down, take off your shoes, loosen your clothes, and create a "vacation within." Breathe deeply and slowly until a warm heaviness suffuses your body. Now imagine yourself relaxing in your favorite vacation spot. Perhaps you are lying on the beach in Hawaii with the sun shining down, surf rolling in, and a gentle breeze blowing through your hair. By letting your imagination go for ten minutes or more, you will be able to leave troublesome worries behind and enjoy a soothing calm.

* See Harold H. Bloomfield and Robert Kory, *The Holistic Way to Health and Happiness.* Simon & Schuster, New York, 1978.

•Another widely used relaxation technique is called Jacobson's Progressive Muscular Relaxation. What distinguishes this technique from others is the careful attention you must pay to relaxing each major muscle group at a time. Begin with your hand as follows:

—Clench your hand into a fist, as tight as you can. Hold the tension for a few seconds. Feel the tightness of the muscles.
—Now let go. Let your hand relax. Feel the warmth and calm suffuse your palm and fingers.
—Keep your attention on your hand muscles for another minute or two. Your awareness will help the relaxation deepen until your hand is completely relaxed.

•Each muscle group must be fully relaxed before you go on to another. To relax your entire body apply the above three steps of tension-release-awareness to each of your muscle groups as follows:

—Dominant hand and forearm
—Dominant upper arm
—Non-dominant hand and forearm
—Non-dominant upper arm
—Forehead
—Eyes and nose
—Cheeks and mouth
—Neck and throat
—Chest, back, and respiratory muscles
—Abdomen
—Dominant upper leg, calf, and foot
—Non-dominant upper leg, calf, and foot

The whole practice can be done lying down or sitting in a comfortable table chair, and will take approximately twenty to thirty minutes.

•Cardiologist Herbert Benson has developed a summary derivative of various ancient and modern relaxation techniques. Popularized through his book *The Relaxation Response*, the process involves four steps:

—Sit comfortably in a quiet room.

—Close your eyes.
—Relax your muscles systematically, starting with your feet, and work up to your head.
—Repeat the word "one" (or any simple word or syllable you might choose) to yourself with each exhalation.

The Benson technique is often not as simple as is claimed. Meditation is traditionally considered a process that requires expert personal instruction for maximum benefit and understanding.

•Meditation is the oldest and perhaps most effective technique for experiencing the healing silence. While there are many meditation techniques that you might learn, you should recognize that the techniques vary in important ways, such as the ease of practice, the amount of time required for results, and the availability of qualified instructors.

•Among the various meditation techniques, consider TM. It is easy to learn and practice. The benefits of the TM program have been established by modern scientific research, and skilled instructors are available at TM centers in most major cities. A qualified TM teacher can help you experience deep levels of the healing science.

WHEN THE NEED FOR PSYCHOTHERAPY?

- If your love relationships are repeatedly frustrating.

- If you're not feeling good about yourself most of the time.

- If you're seeking solace in a liquor bottle, drugs, or a make-believe world.

- If growing up is hard to do, and you're still emotionally fixated on parental love. For example, the need for a mother's perpetual admiration or a father's approval.

- If you feel blocked off from your feelings or feel under perpetual strain.

- When you're in a severe emotional crisis, and wise friends and family support won't do.

- If you're not living up to your potentialities and want more out of life.

- You may not need psychotherapy, only a consultation or two.

- Seek out competent help; most people spend more time buying a car than looking for the right therapist! Check with your family physician, mental health agencies—shop wisely.

THE THERAPEUTIC PROCESS

•Psychotherapy aims at helping a person develop a warm, accepting attitude toward himself and others. Blocks to self-love and love of others are gradually removed through corrective emotional experiences.

•The neurotic individual requires self-love to become well. A wise therapist will use every opportunity for ego-building to help the person feel more pleasure and respect for himself.

•The personal characteristics of the therapist are more important than brand of therapy (Transactional Analysis, Gestalt, Reality Therapy, etc.) in determining therapeutic goals. Depending on the therapist's orientation, estimates may vary. Don't expect overnight miracles, or years of uncertain squandering of time and money.

•The burden of making positive changes will still be upon you. You can expect your therapist to be kindly and patient, but he will not treat you as sick, defective, or about to fall apart.

•Therapy at its best is a good model of a loving (but not sexual) relationship. Contacts with the therapist should leave you feeling more hopeful and with greater self-esteem; not worse than before.

GUIDELINES FOR CHANGE

• Whether in therapy or on your own the key is to take more responsibility, indeed the opportunity, for developing your own happiness and well-being. Don't just be a complainer. Complaining puts tremendous pressure on those around you and makes you hard to live with. You have the power to become the person you want to be.

• Make a plan, establish priorities. Don't set your goals too high. Favor making positive change, rather than just focusing on the negative. Keep a chart or a self-improvement diary.

• Move one step at a time. You can't solve all your problems at once. Trying to do too much too soon is a sure way to meet failure and frustration. Have patience. Systematically follow the steps in this book that apply to you, and your happiness will grow steadily.

• If you are receiving medical care or psychotherapy integrate your own efforts with the care and advice of your doctor. Establish an adult-adult health partnership, for change is primarily up to you.

• Enlist the support of family members and friends. No one can more quickly undermine a program for change than an uncooperative spouse. People going through changes together (losing weight, a fitness program, greater assertiveness) can support and encourage one another.

- Recognize that plateaus will occur. Change occurs in stages of rest and activity, sometimes one step backward for every two steps forward. The body, mind, or a relationship does not readjust in a smooth and continuous fashion. Don't be discouraged; stay with your improvement plan. Plateaus are natural to progress.

SELF-MASTERY

•Mastery doesn't mean learning to tightly suppress your feelings. To the contrary, it involves acceptance and freedom for all of your emotions, with the ability to keep them under reasonable control. Self-mastery will enable you to deal with high-voltage situations in an objective and compassionate manner.

•Self-indulgence and uncontrolled hedonism can produce self-hate. Self-discipline with your lower-self needs (gentle firmness, never ruthless suppression) will create self-affirmation, a deepening appreciation of yourself and others.

•Self-mastery connotes taking responsibility for your emotions, for no one else can cause them. "You make me uptight" or "You hurt me" is blaming others for emotions that are within you. Instead, try asking yourself why you feel uptight or hurt when you're in these situations. Further growth and openness then become possible. Every emotional reaction tells us something more about ourselves.

•Trying to find satisfaction by manipulating others to make the "correct" emotional response is at best a precarious situation—you win some and you lose some. And you're more than likely to zero in on what you don't have with anger, fear, or jealousy.

•Learn to enjoy all that you do have; strive for self-sufficiency. Get out of the ego game of having to have A,B,C in order to be happy. It would be nice perhaps to have A or B or C, but not necessary.

•We are never satisfied until we become our best self. The nature of the mind is to want more and more. The real treasures which we seek are not in our neighbor's possessions or the envy of others, but in fulfilling our latent potentialities.

•Don't try to tell others to be more loving; let your life bespeak your love. Work on yourself, grow in happiness, and others will naturally begin to tune in to their higher potentialities.

CULTIVATE PREFERENCES

•Your happiness and equanimity are tenuous as long as you foster emotion-backed demands. Most of us tend to blame others for the emotional upsets we have: "Stop making me feel guilty" or, "If you wouldn't be late I wouldn't be so angry." Or perhaps we blame the environment: "It rained for two weeks; I had an awful vacation."

•We can spend our energies becoming better wheeler-dealers, manipulators, trying to fulfill our list—often conflicting—of emotion-backed demands, but this style is shallow and limiting. A style of milder preferences makes for less anger and frustration, more flexibility and freedom.

•Preference instead of demand of expectation means you might prefer to have Italian instead of Chinese food, prefer to have sex tonight, but if you have Chinese food and your wife's not in a sexual mood it doesn't matter, there is no disappointment, your inner flow of happiness remains untouched.

•For the sake of your own happiness as well as that of others, cultivate maximum flexibility. A late appointment or burned toast is never worth you losing your love and equanimity.

•When we go with the flow and stop trying so hard, we find that our desires spontaneously become fulfilled. Learn to just take it as it comes, to neither anticipate nor resist change. You'll begin to innocently enjoy each new situation as it unfolds.

FINDING YOUR DHARMA

•*Dharma* is an Indian word meaning "that which upholds." To find your dharma means to find that field of activity which is most smoothly in accord with your deepest and highest nature.

•Established in your dharma, your actions will be like a powerful current which forcibly carries with it all that comes in its path. Success will "come naturally," in accord with the noblest principles of life.

•Your creative energies need channeling. Gas by itself does nothing; it needs a combustion engine. Music is the revelation of silence made audible. Growth is disciplined; creative energy expresses itself best in focused activity.

•Without an outlet unfulfilled potential produces suffering, for the power behind human evolution is great. Develop your talent, no matter how many years the training or what the obstacle.

•When our activities suit our style and temperament, it produces maximum results for ourselves and others. If our actions do not suit our temperament or inclination we experience strain and boredom; work becomes a drag.

LOVE'S LABOR

•Do what you love and you will do it well. Only work done with love is done optimally, whether one is a gas station attendant or a surgeon. Work is not just the technical skills we perform, but the kind of energy-environment we create around us and those we serve.

•The design for success in the marketplace has required the manipulation of feelings, the denial of love. The concern of most people with accumulating more material goods has become a substitute for affection. But of what value is success in the marketplace if we are not successful with others or ourselves?

•We are frequently raised to think we have to manipulate, compete, and twist our way to success, that the success and love compartments of life just don't mix. A compulsive drive for more power and security without a concomitant growth of the heart, brings with it anxiety neurosis, peptic ulcers, and heart disease.

•Business in its highest sense consists of transactions that are mutually satisfying, mutually enhancing. The unconditional love of everyone around you—in your personal and business life—will open more doors and gain you greater success than, for example, "winning through intimidation." Whether you are a corporate executive, army sergeant or teacher, if you behave in a reassuring and caring manner, the people under you will not only show improved mental health but superior performance.

•The goal should be a twofold process—inner growth giving rise to external achievement, which then stimulates once again inner development. Like that, we can spiral to higher and higher levels of fulfillment. Our sphere of influence grows in consonance with the growth of our consciousness.

SEARCH FOR EXCELLENCE

•Anything you do, from decorating your house to managing a business, becomes artistry if motivated by the passion for excellence and stamped with your personal style. It also makes any task more satisfying.

•The torch of life has been passed to you, make it burn as brightly as possible. One such as you will never pass this way again. You are unique, one of a kind. Fulfill your talents to the utmost!

•Advance in the direction of your ideals. There is a strong likelihood for each of us to become what we imagine ourselves to be. Dream castles in the sky are uplifting. Now build a foundation under them.

•Faith in oneself is the key to success, courage its handmaiden. Trials and tribulations are to make, not break, you. A life worth living is not one that is easy, but one that is full.

•Sometimes we have to take risks, go for the long shot. If the tree is sturdy and the branch strong, why not go out on a limb—that's where the fruit is! What better person to bet on than you.

•Do not aim to just maintain, but to surpass yourself. Spend your life on something that will outlast you. Keep faith in the highest destiny of man.

SUCCESS

That man is a success who has lived well, laughed often and loved much; who has gained the respect of intelligent men and the love of children; who has filled his niche and accomplished his task; who leaves the world better than he found it, whether by an improved poppy, a perfect poem or a rescued soul; who never lacked appreciation of earth's beauty or failed to express it; who looked for the best in others and gave the best he had.

Robert Louis Stevenson

LOVE BLOSSOMS IN THE SOIL OF HAPPINESS

•The seed of love grows in the soil of happiness. The fruits of love are the natural result of the expansion of happiness.

•A classic misunderstanding held by many is that love leads to happiness. Certainly love can heal, love can motivate anew, but you cannot expect someone to come along and magically transform you into a happy, fulfilled human being. You must provide a lot of growth from your side; these habits of growth will then naturally lead you to the sharing of love.

•No matter how hard the unhappy person tries to love, his efforts are destined for frustration because he lacks the inner sense of well-being basic to the ability to love. The key to loving is to raise your baseline happiness—your moment-to-moment joy in living, without anything special having to happen, like a great party or a new beau.

•The more at ease you become the more others will find that they rarely get tense when they are with you. Your love and happiness spread to others, it's a contagious effect. Warmth, sharing, and love come naturally to a happy person.

•Real acceptance of others—unconditional love—only becomes possible when your baseline happiness no longer depends on people's behaving in a certain way toward you, when you are so okay inside of yourself that it is all okay, no matter what.

REFINED APPRECIATION

• With a growing baseline happiness, you appreciate life more, and the ultimate development of the ability to appreciate is love. This kind of growth in appreciation will lead you to start having warmer relations with others, and develops naturally into love for oneself, family, friends, the environment, and all humanity.

• A loving cycle ensues: The more appreciation you feel, the more love you radiate, the more love you will receive in return.

• Fulfillment is not built upon international fame or fabulous vacations, but upon clusters of daisies and flocks of geese noticed by the wayside. As the windows of perception are cleansed, we begin to see the miraculous in the ordinary.

• How full of love can life become? We mustn't judge by people who are restricted in their ability to love, for they are like small ponds where the love can flow only as ripples, not as huge waves in the ocean.

• As a person's capacity to appreciate unfolds, he lives in an unbounded flow of love at the sight, sound, taste, and smell of everything. Our capacity for love is infinite.

ATTRACTIVENESS

•A major barrier to the flow of love in our society is our marketplace orientation. Attractiveness has come to mean whatever package of physical, personality, and social factors is currently in *Vogue*—literally. We tend to desire and reject one another like objects, in a programmed fashion.

•Most people follow several variations of the same path in their quest to become more lovable:

- More power and wealth
- Cultivating one's dress, physique, and hairdo
- Developing a "good personality," "sex appeal," and "popularity"

•At the end of struggle and strain for this commercially packaged rainbow, too many people are finding not a pot of gold but bankruptcy. It is high time we search for beauty that is more than skin deep.

•Remember: There is nothing more attractive than a naturally happy, fulfilled, alive human being. Cheerfulness and contentment are great beautifiers.

•That's not to say you shouldn't look your best, carry yourself assertively, exercise regularly, or enjoy the latest fashions. It's just that inner radiance comes first.

THE RIGHT MODEL

• It is very important to have a clear vision of the possibilities, a model of a healthy, fully functioning human being.

• Unfortunately, many of us have not been exposed to a fully loving person in our childhood.

• Entering adolescence, we choose a movie star, rock singer, or football player as our role model. The ideal becomes the headliner: power, fame, or good looks instead of outstanding qualities of heart and mind.

• Culturally and individually we must be very careful whom we hold up for admiration and recognition, for especially in our formative years we learn a great deal from modeling.

• The gentleman, the hero, the mystic, the knight have all fallen by the wayside. Our culture is in need of a superior vision of our human capacity.

• We must expose ourselves and our youth to the very best of our species; the loving, contented person, though he is not a headliner. We in the chain of humanity have been taught that we are as weak as our weakest link. This is but half the truth, points out Kahlil Gibran. We are also as strong as our strongest link.

SELF-ACTUALIZATION

•Abraham Maslow† described some of the characteristics of the fully healthy, self-actualized human being:

- –Clearer, more efficient perception of reality
- –More openness to experience
- –Greater freshness of appreciation
- –Increased integration, wholeness, unity of the person
- –Increased spontaneity, expressiveness, aliveness
- –A real self; firm identity; autonomy; uniqueness
- –A resistance to enculturation
- –Increased objectivity; detachment; transcendence of self
- –Greatly increased creativeness
- –Ability to fuse concreteness and abstractness
- –Democratic character structure
- –Improved interpersonal relationships
- –Ability to love

† Abraham Maslow, *Toward a Psychology of Being*. D. Van Nostrand Company, New York, 1968.

THE LOVING PERSON

•If one grows to one's fullest human potentiality, the ability to love will spontaneously blossom. The fully developed human being emanates love just as naturally as he emits kindness or autonomy.

•The capacity to give and receive love is the major criterion of mental health. Love in its most mature sense is a way of life.

•Qualities of the loving person:

- –High baseline happiness (an unshakable enjoyment of living)
- –Respects and appreciates self and others
- –Innocent and open
- –Spontaneously giving
- –Self-sufficient
- –Fully alive, great vitality
- –Tuned in to the desires of others
- –Enriches the lives of those around him
- –Spontaneous right action
- –Flexible and adaptable
- –Unconditional, can risk disappointment
- –Freely moves between union and separation, partnership and individuation
- –Kind and just
- –Helpful and responsible
- –Harmonizing, thoughtful
- –Universal in scope

THE WORLD IS AS YOU ARE

•If we have fear inside, it is a fearful, mistrustful world. If we are filled with love and serenity, it is a joyful world.

•The mind cannot maintain a mood on an abstract basis. A person cannot for long feel fear, anger, or even joy without his mind searching for some explanation.

•The person who complains that life has no purpose, that nothing is worthwhile, is projecting his boredom, apprehension, and poor self-esteem. This projective mechanism was described long before Sigmund Freud, by Charles Dickens: "Men who look on nature and their fellow men, and cry that all is gloomy are in the right; but the sombre colours are reflections from their own jaundiced eyes and hearts. The real hues are delicate, and need a clearer vision."

•A loving person lives in a world full of happy people not only because of the love and happiness he radiates, but because he brings out happiness in others. Even those people who are angry and depressed experience temporary joy in his presence. He responds to, and therefore brings out, the best and highest in others.

•As you become more loving, you will find the world to be a friendly, loving place that is designed to give you all that you may need. The Garden of Eden is right here on earth waiting to be rediscovered.

BIRDS OF A FEATHER FLOCK TOGETHER

•As children, our environment expresses our parents' thinking, but gradually we break away to create an experiential universe of our own. Entering adulthood, our social relationships directly reflect our level of consciousness; we make our own worlds.

•"You are what you eat"—not just nutritionally, but also intellectually, emotionally, and socially. Let yourself flow to those people and that environment which brings out the best in you.

•Healthy individuals are very perceptive in judging others. This awareness shows up in forming friendships, business alliances, or choosing a marital partner. Neurotic people, stunted in their own growth, are overshadowed by their neediness, frequently choosing one "loser" after another. While the healthy person's love is discriminating and accurate, the neurotic's love is truly blind.

•Therefore, it is more important to be the right person than to find the right person. You will naturally meet beautiful, loving people as you develop the love within you. Likes attract likes; happiness attracts most powerfully of all.

•Unfold your fullest powers; nature will direct you to your true love's door.

SHARING

—Staying in Love
—Communication Skills
—Effective Listening
—Feedback
—Favor Positivity
—Friendship
—Maleness/Femaleness
—Your Heart Line
—The Ethics of Love
—Timing
—Anaclitic and Narcissistic Love
—The Romantic Urge to Marry
—Marital Readiness
—Selecting a Partner
—Two Halves Don't Make a Whole
—Commitment
—Like "Pillars of the Temple"
—Marital Style
—Happily Ever After
—Chronic Enjoyment
—Being-together
—Love, Work, and Play
—Freedom and Jealousy
—Relationship Crises
—Marital Therapy
—Sensitivity Training
—Nude Dialogue
—Non-verbal Exercises
—Massage
—Your Love Sanctuary
—Love's Play
—Love vs. Lust
—Sexual Health
—Sexual Dysfunction
—Sexual Fantasy
—X-rated, In-joy
—Multi-orgasm for Two
—Spiritual Love-making
—Tantra
—Conceived and Received with Love
—Love: The Essential Nutrition
—Freud Was Right
—Too Much Love?
—The Children of Tomorrow
—Your Family Roots

STAYING IN LOVE

- A happy relationship depends upon each partner entering the relationship with a strong baseline happiness.

- If a person is already enjoying considerable pleasure from within, pleasure derived from a relationship becomes an added delight. He is not dependent upon the other for a stable sense of self, for inner fulfillment.

- This autonomy frees both people from the need of making escalating demands upon one another to sustain their happiness, and it protects them from overwhelming disappointment and anger if a need or expectation goes unmet.

- Each person is free to express his or her full potential instead of feeling trapped by an exclusive dependence on one another for emotional well-being.

- Growth of the other is enjoyed and appreciated, not feared or resented. Let's take a detailed look, in the pages that follow, at the means to achieving greater happiness in your relations.

COMMUNICATION SKILLS

•We humans are as if encapsulated, isolated in our small, semipermeable shells. Communication is an opportunity to greet one another, to bridge the pangs of separation with love and unity.

•Communication is more than the exchange of words, it is the sharing of ourselves. Such a communion requires first of all being open to our inner voice, our inner cues: "Yes, I really do want to," "Why am I so tired?" "I enjoy being with you." Being fully in touch with your feelings is a prerequisite to experiencing the feelings of others.

•Change occurs in small, steady increments. "Improving the relationship" is too global. Better to improve your communication skills in a steady, step-by-step manner. Do so early, before poor habits and a slush fund (backlog of negative emotions) accrue.

•The goal is not to think and act alike, but to think and share together. Loved ones can strongly disagree on almost any subject, yet still deepen in their love for one another.

•Great differences can be supported when emotional ease prevails. Calmness of mind even at a heated moment allows for an underlying sense of love, respect, and harmony.

•In an atmosphere of trust our hidden feelings can emerge—the guilts, fears, shames, and inhibitions that we have been hiding from ourselves. Sharing these feelings freely and completely as they emerge helps us to better accept ourselves. Trust that underneath the anger, the hurt, and the shame is love.

• Help each other to fully accept your bodies, feelings, and thoughts. The positive regard and acceptance of the loved one can help emotional blocks to melt away. Love's stumbling blocks are best removed with love.

EFFECTIVE LISTENING

•We show our understanding more by the way we listen than the words we say. Don't interrupt, or offer glib suggestions or ready-made solutions. By your presence you say, "I'm totally available to you, my mind and heart are yours."

•Effective listening is discovering. Rather than saddle someone with pearls of advice, listen attentively and with acceptance. People will find their own right way and ask for advice when needed.

•Effective listening is being concentrated into the here-and-now, not caught up in cocktail-party mannerisms. We listen with our third ear and see with our third eye; we bear a loving, non-judgmental witness.

•A divided mind, being in a situation but with your mind somewhere else, produces exhaustion and tension. Concentrated listening will energize and uplift both you and your party. Your mind will be calm, allowing you to be patient and then to respond appropriately.

•You can feel compassion without getting entangled in the emotional predicaments of others. People must walk their own path; learn their lessons for themselves. Lend a helping hand, but recognize that each of us must awaken at our own rate and time.

FEEDBACK

•Avoid globally judgmental statements as "You're never on time" or "You don't love me." Better are such specific feeling statements as "What happened? . . . I get frustrated when I'm left waiting" or "I feel unloved. I could use a hug."

•Learn to discuss grievances rather than pout; have feedback sessions. Yelling, pouting, and name-calling are not feedback. Feedback is above all constructive, sincerely aimed at helping the other person to grow.

•Feedback is in the "now"—not pulling out a nasty from ten years ago. Feedback is accurate. Instead of saying, "You're a fool," say, "I think you're mistaken. Roses are red, violets are blue."

•Share your anger or disappointment with work, consumer prices, or the stock market. Don't vent your irritation on your spouse. If your boss yells at you, don't go home and kick your wife. Kick your boss!

•More seriously, give appropriate feedback to your boss instead: "I wish you wouldn't yell at me. I respond to criticism much better when it is given to me in a supportive way. The error in question will be taken care of. With assistance from you I hope to do better next time."

•Be kind and loving when offering feedback. "You don't pay any attention to me" delivered in a hostile fashion just stokes the fires, while "Dear, do you like me in this outfit? I'd like to turn you on," is more likely to inspire.

• Catch the person at the right time: not at the end of a long, hard day but after his evening meditation. Or talk softly and gently after giving a scalp or neck massage. The emotional climate—not just your words—is the key.

• Of course, you yourself must be open to feedback. Learn to not feel hurt but to value constructive criticism. Honest feelings from others help you to understand how others perceive you. As a result you improve your interpersonal style.

FAVOR POSITIVITY

• You can work wonders by overlooking the negative statements of others, while never failing to appreciate their good deeds. Positive stroking, a smile or kind word, is more potent than provoking or wielding power.

• For a couple that has fallen into bad habits, a good exercise is for each of you to list on a piece of paper ten specific things which you like about the other. Items must be positive as well as specific. Example: "I enjoyed our walk through the park last Sunday, talking with you about my hassles at work. That was very meaningful to me." Exchange papers and then discuss each item for a few minutes. Keep to the positive only.

• Strive to be good-humored, considerate, optimistic, patient, and forgiving with regard to each other's weaknesses and imperfections. As Confucius say: "Better to light one small candle than to curse the darkness."

• Most of us like not only to be loved but also to be told we are loved. Tell her tonight how much you hold her dear. Compliment a job well done or an outfit worn well. Share a heartfelt kiss and hug.

• Mark Twain used to say that he could live for two months on a good compliment. He never did say whether it was one he received or one he gave. Kind words produce positivity not only in the recipient, but also in the sender.

• Talk happiness. No road is wholly rough; look for the places that are smooth and clear. Talk health. An endless description of aches and pains charms no one. Favor wellness and soon it will be so.

FRIENDSHIP

•It is a great joy—indeed essential—to have at least one human being whom we can utterly trust with the deepest murmurings of our soul, one who knows the best and the worst of us and yet loves us through and through.

•A friend: one who doesn't simply flatter but who speaks the truth, who lends support and encouragement during difficult times as well as celebrates our good fortune.

•Honor thy friendships. "Do not," as the ancient Chinese admonish, "remove a fly from a friend's forehead with a hatchet." Use an ostrich feather instead.

•"A friend," says Robert Louis Stevenson, "is a present you give yourself." We get the friends and lovers we deserve.

•Many believe that being a good pal and being a spouse or lover are mutually exclusive, if not contradictory. This is just not so. A comfortable sharing is essential to any love relationship. Lovers had better not just love but also like one another!

MALENESS/FEMALENESS

•While it is important to feel confident in one's maleness or femaleness, it is best not to have expectations or prescriptions as to the role of the sexes. How unfortunate that we have locked our human potential into frozen and stereotypic patterns.

•Becoming a neurosurgeon or balancing a checkbook, cooking dinner or running a corporation, weaving rugs or jogging—are abilities and responsibilities that belong to both sexes.

•Some men—and women—may find women's liberation initially quite threatening, but at the core of this movement lies the liberation of the person. The goal is not to go from one locked-in set of behavioral choices to another: from distraught housewife to liberated woman or from a male chauvinist pig to a with-it bisexual.

•A liberated man is not just one who is willing to change his fair share of the diapers—that would be missing the point—but one who is capable of providing his wife and child with the full tenderness, respect, and care each is due.

•The idea is for each person to become all that he is capable of becoming without sex role constraints or limitations. But more than that, both sexes must aim for a higher integration of seemingly opposite values. Passive/active, gentle/strong, child-rearing /world-moving, sex roles can be transcended toward the greater ennoblement of us all.

•Presently, an overbalance of harsh willfulness still predominates in the world. Men must learn to share their power as they regain the joys of tenderness, ecstasy, and wonder. Women's might and wisdom are penetrating the world's labyrinth of politics and power. The resulting union will bear the fruits of greater love and harmony for all.

YOUR HEART LINE

•All the loves parading through your life are not a play of chance, but links in the chain of the evolution of your heart. Our heart line becomes disentangled as consciousness expands, and our desires become more life-supporting.

•Instead of being a tug-of-war game of female cunning versus male machismo, pre-marital relationships can be a time of great sharing. Don't be attached to marriage as the end-all, which makes dating or a friendship worthwhile. Take it as it comes; enjoy each person fully.

•Honesty is essential. Hidden agendas result in hurt feelings. Don't encourage false expectations to please. Be honest about "where you're coming from" and the chances are greater of meeting someone who has needs complementary to yours.

•When a relationship is not meant to last, learn to lovingly let go. After the hurt and hate, you'll see that change and separation are inevitable to life. The relationship brought you a great deal of good, that's why you'll miss it so.

•Relationships have their beginning, middle, and end, but the love that sustains them goes on forever. You are a richer, deeper person for having loved.

•Complete your mourning. For a while, don't become involved in an all-consuming passionate relationship—let yourself heal. Soon you'll feel whole; new vistas of love shall await you.

THE ETHICS OF LOVE

- The morality of sexual relations before, in, or outside marriage must be judged according to the specifics of a given situation. Quick, harsh black-and-white judgments frequently fade in the light of day. Of crucial importance is the over-all well-being and growth of the sexually involved individuals.

- Sex should be enriching to both parties; life-supporting and joyous. Responsibility, integrity, and care may be more significant determinants of human welfare than whether a given affair is pre- or extra-marital.

- This should not be seen as an endorsement of pre- or extra-marital relations, but rather to emphasize a concern for human values. Certainly the welfare of significant others besides the lovers must be considered, as well as spiritual issues of growth.

- Pre- or post-, extra- or exclusive, homosexual or heterosexual, libertarian or life-celibate—an overriding issue is that love reign supreme.

- As you mature you will undoubtedly find that the pleasures of marriage, faithfulness, and devotion are of the very highest kind. Love can ripen and bear its sweetest fruit within the protective boundaries of a long-term intimate relationship. When marriage grows in its joys, sexual exclusivity becomes more easy.

TIMING

•A critical factor in any relationship is timing. For a relationship to work not only must personalities match but both people must be at the right stage of their individual development.

•You may find yourself rushing into romantic attachments too soon after a separation or divorce. Love on the rebound can have negative consequences.

•Give yourself time to properly heal your previous loss.‡ If your healing hasn't been completed, an initial rebound is likely to be followed by yet another loss.

•Anger and resentment from your previous relationship are likely to spill over. You're still incomplete. Take time to rest your emotions; become whole.

•Falling "madly in love" soon after a traumatic break-up may seem ecstatic for a while: Your wildest fantasies come true. But suddenly the bottom falls out. You discover your new love is not the totally sensuous, sophisticated, intelligent, considerate god/goddess you initially perceived. You've now got two losses to mourn.

‡ For more detail see Melba Colgrove, Harold H. Bloomfield, and Peter McWilliams, *How to Survive the Loss of a Love*. Simon & Schuster, New York, 1976.

ANACLITIC AND NARCISSISTIC LOVE

•Infantile forms of love can inhibit maturation. Some individuals are so hungry for affection that they will "love" anyone who will give them praise and support. Freud called this desire for a surrogate mother or father anaclitic love.

•Others must compulsively rebel, and look for a loved person who has characteristics precisely the opposite of mother. For example, a man harboring hate or feeling tied to his brunette mother, may find brunettes unattractive; compulsively only like blondes. A girl rebelling from a rich, successful father, may seek out only those on the social fringe or failures.

•Narcissism is another important operant in love choice, finding someone who is very much like oneself. Similar qualities looked for may be appearance, intellect, ideals, or special problems (such as drug abuse or alcoholism).

•Even mature love contains some anaclitic and narcissistic elements. A healthy person looks for some love in return, sustenance, support, and praise, but this is far from a clinging dependency. Similarly on the narcissistic side, ever notice how many couples have a similar appearance, or even how a pet dog may be a lookalike!

•As we mature, we become less tied to our infantile needs. We gain increasing degrees of freedom and discrimination. In our love choices, qualities of heart and mind supersede the physical or economic. Similarity on a surface level becomes less important than being alike deep down within.

THE ROMANTIC URGE TO MARRY

•"Stars and rockets" romance has become almost prerequisite for a modern-day marriage. What's all too frequently called "love" at the altar, but is mostly infatuation, romance, or sexual attraction, is not the marital panacea some might hope it to be.

•The inflated importance of romantic love undoubtedly contributes to the failure of so many marriages. A romantic underpinning can certainly hold a couple together long enough to get married, but this is a poor basis if there are no real grounds for a lasting marriage.

•A healthy choice requires your not decorating the beloved with illusory values. The heat of passion can color your senses and good judgment. Passion bubbles burst, giving rise to disappointment and frustration.

•To be real and lasting, love must be felt in the quiet of the living room, not just in the passion of the bedroom. There must be spiritual, mental, and social harmony.

•Marriage is for a long time, as much as twenty-four hours a day! Ask yourself: Is this the person I can most be myself with? Do we communicate well together? Are our goals, values, and aspirations in tune? Do we *like* each other? What do our friends and families say?

•For better and for worse we learn primarily through modeling. Psychologically speaking, girls frequently grow up to be like their mothers and boys like their fathers. The exceptions are many, but please, if you don't like your future mother- or father-in-law, watch out!

MARITAL READINESS

•There is more to marital readiness than a blood test! How lamentable that we spend so many years training for a professional career and prepare naught for the surpassingly important career of marriage.

•Haste makes waste. A hasty courtship can sometimes lead to awful entanglements. Delaying marriage—by choice or circumstances (such as financial or educational)—is usually beneficial. The passage of time dispels a false infatuation, while it tempers and hones a true spiritual affinity.

•The number one predictor of marital happiness is the happiness of one's parents' marriage. Especially if you come from an unhappy family, raise your baseline happiness first.

•Trying to escape from an unhappy home into marriage is often like jumping from the proverbial frying pan into the fire. Better than 50 per cent of teen-age marriages end in divorce. At the time of marriage, the more mature and differentiated you are, the more durable is your union.

•Your choice in a mate might be very different after you've stabilized and matured. Complete your education, explore your talents, see the world. Unfold your latent potentialities, then consider marriage.

•The need of the times is for strong individuals first, then strong marriages will follow. Strength begets strength, self-actualizing individuals make for a creative and powerful marriage.

SELECTING A PARTNER

• While a person may be attracted to many members of the opposite sex, with maturation the number of potential lovers narrows. He or she can more globally love larger numbers of people, but there is greater differentiation in selecting a potential mate.

• External characteristics, whether these be physical beauty or common interests, may initiate attraction—this is normal and natural—but should never end the process. For a relationship to deepen there must be appreciation for the person as a whole.

• With maturity, values deepen. Characteristics such as kindness, dedication, and basic goodness supersede whether the person is "handsome," "gorgeous," or "stacked." Likewise, differences in background, social class, and education become of less importance than personality traits such as compassion, compatibility, and respect.

• Intellectual and emotional rapport are of high significance. The experience of the man who discovers that he has married a woman with nothing about her head but hair, even of the most soft and golden kind, is a pitiable condition. Similarly, the woman who finds her prize financial-whiz husband incapable of enduring warmth, has gained herself an uninviting and illusory security. For success and fulfillment in marriage, select a mate with a highly developed mind and heart.

• Of course, being a good match is not the only consideration. Let's not forget the vital chemistry of love. For while all the pieces may fit together, love is what binds two people together and makes the marital machine run.

TWO HALVES DON'T MAKE A WHOLE

- A mate or partner is sometimes selected in an attempt to achieve wholeness.

- This may lead to treating the other person like a part of us, not a person in their own right.

- One person may then become threatened by his or her partner's growth. What is experienced by one as a positive change is perceived by the other with fear or envy.

- In a mature love one's individuality is not lost but steadily nurtured. Each partner experiences freedom, independence, and integrity.

- It's beautiful to need one another, but remember, wholeness comes mainly from within.

- Two halves make two halves. Two wholes allow love's fulfillment.

COMMITMENT

- Do not prematurely commit yourself to a love relationship. An immature person may promise lasting love under the heat of passion but have serious regrets the next morning. Strive for honesty in all your relationshiops to avoid causing pain to others . . . and yourself.

- Marriage is more than a honeymoon, it is a lifetime contract. Through thick and thin, for richer and for poorer, marriage requires devotion, a mature ability to commit.

- Be doubly sure before you sign on the dotted line. Have talks with yourself, lover, friends, and family. Invite and be open to feedback. A potential lifetime deal is nothing to be impulsive about!

- The ability to commit depends on many factors, the most significant of which is the degree to which we felt accepted as a child and found value in permanence and stability of our own childhood family relationships. Constancy of love also depends upon the degree of satisfaction in a relationship, both real and as measured by our expectations.

- Nowadays we have a tendency to run off to divorce courts too quickly. Not that two people must consign themselves to embittered and despairing lives (horrors!), but emotionally flat or unrewarding periods are sometimes inevitable. Better to tap your ingenuity, personal resources, or professional help before you throw in the towel.

• Underneath that anger and disappointment is a lot of love. Give a relationship you've already invested so much in your best. No matter which way it goes you'll feel better for having given it your maximum.

LIKE "PILLARS OF THE TEMPLE"

•Growth does not stop when we marry. Each mate has an inherent need to grow.

•Marital partners do not necessarily grow and change in synchrony. One may be happy with the status quo, while the other seeks further horizons.

•A strong sense of autonomy is not only compatible with a successful relationship, but a strong contributant. Persons with highly developed individuality need each other less, but paradoxically, feel free to love each other more. Neither partner is restricted by personal insecurities. They can share great closeness, yet can easily move apart.

•Strive for a relationship of equals. Each responsible for his own happiness, loved and supported by the other. Do your thing but don't impose it on the other. Give to each other the space that you need.

•Love is allowing each person—especially the one you marry—to unfold in his own way, loving them as they are each step of the way.

•As Kahlil Gibran* wrote of marriage, "Give your hearts, but not into each other's keeping . . . and stand together yet not too near together: for the pillars of the temple stand apart, and the oak tree and the cypress grow not in each other's shadow."

* Kahlil Gibran, *The Prophet.* Alfred A. Knopf, New York, 1976, p. 16.

MARITAL STYLE

•The idea of maintaining a marriage of mutual tolerance and convenience, or as a façade of respectability for the sake of children, church, or state, is rapidly declining. Today people marry and stay married chiefly for personal growth and fulfillment. As a result, marital and family styles are rapidly evolving to meet the changing needs of individuals.

•Many different kinds of union between (or among) people are emerging: open, closed, or group marriage, nuclear and extended family, serial monogamy, communal living, collective child-rearing.

•Exclusive need not mean possessive.
Open need not mean promiscuous.
Closed need not mean stilted.
Freedom need not mean reckless.
Concern need not mean suffocation.
Devotion need not mean servitude.

•The style of marriage should reflect the background, needs and expectations of the partners—not something arbitrarily chosen.

•A healthy marriage changes shape and form to meet the needs of the individuals. The important thing is that a change in style not reflect a loss of love, but love overflowing.

HAPPILY EVER AFTER

•Marriage depends for its aliveness on a healthy emotion of love. A marriage that depends too long upon compulsion or duty soon withers and dies.

•Two persons who marry should recognize that the first flush of physical attraction is far from being the full fruition of love. The initial pleasures come easy; deeper, more lasting pleasures take time.

•Love is something that matures as the result of years of mutual cooperation, the sharing of good times and bad. The fruits of marriage sometimes must go through a long, hot summer and a cold, blustery winter, before they ripen, then sweeten.

•It is a fallacy that love and sexual pleasures have to dwindle with the years. Boredom and apathy are not inevitable. Your marital love life, like a fine wine, can ripen and grow richer with age.

•Little things make the big difference in keeping a marriage vibrant. Sure, bring home candies, flowers, or, on Sunday morning, lox, bagels, and cream cheese. Be attentive, show you care.

•Expectations must be reasonable, tolerance high. Anaïs Nin points out that men and women must learn "the subtle art of oscillation . . . neither strength nor weakness is a fixed quality. We all have our days of strength and our days of weakness."

•The love which led you to marry must not culminate a love story, but be a start to one. Living happily ever after doesn't have to be a fantasy, but can become a true life adventure!

CHRONIC ENJOYMENT

- The likelihood of deepening love and growing emotional rewards is great when relaxation and ease are a basic bond in the relationship.

- Love relationships built on enjoyments are much more stable than relationships based almost exclusively upon excitements.

- Excitement alone breeds short-lived relationships for the same reason it breeds only short-term happiness. The human nervous system is capable of sustaining only so much excitement before it must switch gears, turn off, and restore depleted energy. Relationships not built—at least in part—on quiet enjoyments must inevitably become insufficiently stimulating.

- Just as individual excitement gives rise to boredom and depression, a thrilling relationship can plummet into frustration and disappointment. Often, the more meteoric the rise, the more meteoric the fall.

- Thoreau pointed out that most people, married or otherwise, "lead lives of quiet desperation." We can change all that. Let's aim for "chronic" enjoyment!

BEING-TOGETHER

•Aim for a balance of rest and activity, enjoyments and excitements. Learn to feel equally comfortable during time spent together and time apart. Love relationships tend to grow cyclically, and flourish amidst rest and activity.

•Each of us needs to learn to not just tolerate, but to enjoy being alone. When you grow comfortable with your aloneness, then you are ready to share.

•Lovers can more deeply appreciate and understand each other when they learn the value of silence. Then a couple can *be* together happily. With each partner established in the silent pleasure of being, the relationship is more likely to blossom. Rainer Maria Rilke put it beautifully: "Love consists in this, that two solitudes protect and touch and greet each other."

•Regular experience of the healing silence (see pages 79–80), helps a couple to maximize their happiness. The tranquility and ease of meditation allow each individual to do their own psychological housecleaning. Instead of venting their stresses upon one another, their activity is infused harmony with love and good cheer.

•Cultivate enjoyments together: partake in some creative work, sports activity, or take walks together. In the age of the automobile the beauty of long walks is in danger of being forgotten. A hike through the woods, or along the beach, is a great opportunity to share your innermost thoughts and dreams.

•Get away from the noisy, odor-filled city. Rediscover the chirping of birds, the rustle of leaves, shimmering icicles in a sunlit forest. Go tree hugging or cotton-cloud watching. Rebalance, rediscover, unwind.

LOVE, WORK, AND PLAY

•Treat your love relations with the greatest of care, as a gardener would tend his roses. When you look back over the years, success and achievements will pale in significance beside your love memories and intimate associations.

•Some people may expect love or marriage to compensate for an emotionally frustrating, demeaning, or boring job. Such an expectation can make a love relationship precarious; tensions from work may quickly spill over. Conversely, persons happy in their career will have more energy to share with their loved ones.

•Practical aspects are important to any relationship. Not only whether you love each other in the abstract sense, but how well you work and play together. Cooperating with household maintenance makes it easier for love to flow.

•Household cares become household joys, when done or shared together. You cut the carrots, I'll make the dressing; you clear the table, I'll wash the dishes: Preparing a meal together is fun. Food cooked with love and eaten with love, nourishes the soul as well as the body.

•Even tasks and responsibilities can have their shared moments of fun and laughter. You can water each other when doing the garden or tell funnies while folding the laundry. Lovers of life—much like children and puppies—take a playful delight in almost everything. Work gets done, efficiently at that, but always with undercurrents of good cheer.

FREEDOM AND JEALOUSY

•When two people in a love relationship are complete within themselves they do not experience the love they have for others as diminishing, detracting, or threatening to the love they share. They are free of the fear and insecurity that give rise to possessiveness or overreactive jealousy.

•The person who strives to absorb or engulf another is not loving too much but loving selfishly and too little. The other person may experience emotional suffocation and suppressed anger at being so "lovingly" manipulated. A beloved must be free to be an individual; if not, a rebellious affair may result.

•Love not freely given is no love at all. If you love because you are afraid that you can't emotionally survive without the other, or just because the other gives love to you, that is love not freely given. Unspoken bargains of "I'll meet your needs if you'll meet mine" are at best a form of mutual satisfaction, not love in its highest form.

•It is an irony that the more possessive you are, the more love you demand, the less you receive, while the more freedom you give, the less you demand, the more love you'll receive. A true love relationship can never be held together by demanding "shoulds" and "should nots." The glue of love is binding, but free.

•Instead of trying to get the other person to conform to the image you have of a lovable person, seek to know them as they are. The more you can turn demands into preferences, the more self-sufficiently happy you become, the more free and fulfilling will your love relationship be.

• No one person can meet all your interpersonal needs. Don't be jealous of your lover's enjoying others. If the relationship is strong you need not fear or be jealous; if it is weak, better to put your energies into strengthening it. Rome did not fall because of invading barbarians, but because of internal weakness.

• A true love relationship becomes spontaneously moral. Just as a river must flow within boundaries, sexual boundaries to a love relationship are important to its growth. These boundaries are best when they are self-imposed, then love can flow more freely.

RELATIONSHIP CRISES

•Almost every relationship has an emotional crisis at one time or another. A crisis is an invitation to mobilize your very best; it is an invitation to growth.

•Don't quit prematurely. An occasional bout of friction or argumentativeness may be a sign of a vibrant relationship. No booze or drugs—they will just complicate things further.

•Let the steam out. Give each other permission to feel angry or hurt. The sooner the boil is lanced, the quicker you can heal.

•Don't keep throwing darts at one another while your defenses are down, your heart bleeding. Everybody loses in the "getting even" game. Take it easy. Allow your emotional hurts to heal.

•You both must ask yourselves what you can do to make the relationship better. If both of you take 100 per cent responsibility upon yourselves, effective dialogue and a commitment to change become possible.

•Just as we had good days and bad, ups and downs, before we got married, so a relationship too can have its moments of tension and boredom. If you had emotional difficulties before, chances are you'll have difficulties after—don't expect marriage to be your ticket to Nirvana.

•You're not the first couple to go through difficult times. Family, friends, or clergy may be helpful.

MARITAL THERAPY

•An ounce of prevention is worth a pound of cure. Pre-marital counseling and classes can be enriching. Take at least as much time to learn about marriage as you do about sailing a boat.

•Pressure-cooker recipes for happiness do not a marriage save. There is no substitute for the growth and maturation of both partners and periodic reassessment of their commitment to one another.

•If your marriage is having difficulties, get help *early!* As with physical disease, the earlier you catch a marriage in trouble, the more can be done about it. The longer you wait, the worse is the prognosis.

•Intimacy difficulties don't magically resolve. Individual or couples therapy may be useful. But, please—when looking for assistance beware of charlatans and amateurs. Seek out competent professional assistance.

SENSITIVITY TRAINING

•In the process of growing up many of us have learned to suppress anger, sadness, or sexual desire because we unconsciously fear that expressing such emotions will somehow be destructive to our own personality or to others.

•Sensitivity training and encounter groups can help you become more sensitive to your emotions and that of others, by encouraging the honest sharing of moment-to-moment feelings in a supportive way.

•Couples sensitivity groups focus especially upon the communication areas of the love relationship. Married and other love—committed partners learn to better handle ambivalent feelings toward one another and to deepen their mutual understanding.

•A word of caution. Part of the intensive group movement has fallen into the hands of faddists and poorly trained group leaders. Poor leadership and no screening can lead to psychological damage. So, please, find yourself a competent group leader.

•A loving couple can do a simple home exercise to strengthen an already solid marriage. Each of you keep a journal in which you record for ten to fifteen minutes daily a free flow of your emotions and inner life. Exchange journals every other day and discuss in depth their contents. Your entries should be vivid and concrete, your discussions non-judgmental.

NUDE DIALOGUE

•Nude dialogue can help a married or very intimate couple add greater depth and honesty to their relationship. In the privacy and comfort of their home the couple sits completely nude, tailor-fashion, approximately six feet apart. This technique is not meant so much as an entree into sexuality as a daily means for developing greater rapport.

•A married couple sitting across the room from each other, fully clothed in their character armor, can try to talk about each other and their relationship incessantly without really opening up. But let them sit naked, facing each other upon the floor, and their souls and honest emotions will more quickly become bared.

•Nudity under proper circumstances is a significant means for getting beyond inhibitions and insecurities. The disrobing helps remove cover-up, hypocrisy, and shame. Not only the body but emotions and the mind are opened up, so true rapport can be gained.

•After the partners get verbally clear, sensitively sharing feedback, communication and the day's events, they come together knee to knee, to hold hands and gaze into each other's eyes. Silence adds heightened dignity to the shared intimacy of these moments. They can lean forward to kiss, stroke one another, or massage. Still later sexual relations become an option.

•The daily practice of nude dialogue not only allows for clearance, but for greater compassion, solemnity, and reverence. This technique is not for those who have too much to hide, who are already crippled by shame and deception. Rather, such dialogue is for loving partners who wish to insure open communication, to further their love and equality.

NON-VERBAL EXERCISES

•Non-verbal exercises can be a beautiful vehicle when words alone do not seem to meet the need. While non-verbal exercises are most often utilized in a therapy context, a healthy couple can use these to further the process of deepening awareness and satisfaction.

•Every couple at one time or another can experience difficulty recognizing and appropriately expressing aggressive feelings. Controlled and stylized pushing can be an effective means for safely channeling hostility. You and your partner should face each other, and clasp both hands palm to palm. Plant your feet to give you leverage and then, when you agree, begin to push each other, attempting to make the other give ground.

•Such programmatic "pushing" allows you to expend some of the physical energy which your anger has aroused. It further provides a feeling of self-control, which will enable you and your partner to then more freely speak about what's bugging you. There has been physical contact between two people who might otherwise have become encapsulated and withdrawn.

•Sometimes it's easier to express hostility toward an inanimate object than interpersonally. Beating a pillow, a couch, or comfortable chair provides a convenient means for achieving self-control and catharsis. As the mood becomes more settled, verbal exploration should follow.

•Even more difficult for some people to express than aggressive feelings is warmth, tenderness, and affection. A hug can provide a warm, concrete demonstration of closeness and support. Try walking slowly toward each other, hold hands; now very slowly embrace. After a few minutes of silent hugging, sit down and express whatever feelings this exercise aroused.

• A hug a day helps keep the doctor (marriage counselor, therapist) away. It helps to dissipate feelings of sadness, loneliness, and despair. Take turns hugging each other; it's great!

MASSAGE

•Apart from sexual interest and gratification, we humans retain a need for tenderness, caressing, and touch. You can bring enormous pleasure to another human being through massage.

•You need not confine massage to those with whom you are sexually involved. You can massage your parents, acquaintances, and friends. Flow with the massage; you'll derive as much from your tender loving care as your partner.

•Massage is easy, as old as human existence. The ingredients are a warm, quiet setting, soft lighting, scented oil (kept warm by using candle heat or a coffee warmer), a firm mattress, soft pillows, or carpet, soothing music or silence (please, take the phone off the hook). Take plenty of time, don't rush.

•Touch continuously in a regular, easy rhythm. Use the full surface of your hands. Keep your fingers together. Develop your personal style, but always stay smooth and symmetrical.

•There are different strokes–circling, pressing, kneading, rotating, shaking, lifting, pulling–for different folks, and for various regions of the body. Use your intuition, but a good massage book† can help.

† Cordon Inkeles and Murray Todris, with photographs by Robert Foothorap, *The Art of Sensual Massage.* Simon & Schuster, New York, 1972.

•Don't neglect any body parts. The head, hands, legs, and feet are all too often neglected. A soft hairbrush, shampooing the scalp, a rolling pin on the back and legs, a vibrator (or two, one on each hand), and an alcohol rub can add special and delightful effects.

•An atmosphere of safety and trust is essential. Never criticize your partner for being "uptight," tense, or guarded. The tension will gradually fade. Help the person see their body as a temple, the container of the soul.

YOUR LOVE SANCTUARY

•Consider setting aside a room or part of a room exclusively for your intimacy and love-sharing. Ideally your love sanctuary could be a separate room or else your bedroom.

•A love nest is a special place for just the two of you. Furnishings should be simple, for the emphasis is on your attunement. As your love grows the atmosphere can become profound and sacred.

•Here are a few suggestions, but let the room be expressive of your own subtleties in taste.

- –Thick, soft carpet, or throw rugs that would allow you to comfortably make love upon.
- –Perhaps a waterbed or a mattress on the floor.
- –Cushions: big and small, soft and firm, a few silk, a few satin.
- –Drapes to maximize privacy but which allow in natural light.
- –Colors: soft but lively.
- –Candles, not big overhead lights. Illumination should be soft and warm, enough to just see each other clearly.
- –Incense: sandalwood or rose, the long-burning kind.
- –Fresh flowers or plants–lots of them.
- –Consider keeping your shoes outside the room.
- –Music: soft and easy, or your favorite piece, with dual headphones and speakers.

•Some might prefer more excitation: bright colors, strobe lights, and erotic posters. Go with your desires but emphasize comfort and intimacy.

•Keep your love nest personal; if possible, put your overnight or family guests somewhere else. This is your room for nude dialogue, massage, and deep intimacy.

LOVE'S PLAY

•Let love flow through all of your activities, don't just try to "make it" in the bedroom. Doing "it" more may lead you to enjoying "it" less, unless your love energy is flowing.

•Love wants to flow, don't keep it localized in your genitals. The sex books are wrong; your whole body can be a primary erogenous zone. It just takes letting go.

•Tenderness is an important ingredient, massage a great vehicle. From head to toe, there is more to making love than genital friction: Try scratching the scalp or rubbing toes.

•Mature sexual behavior is a direct expression of sexual feeling. No need to pretend, perform, or feign some imagined "ideal." Good sex is what's good for you and your partner. How often doesn't matter.

•Give yourself and your partner permission to enjoy. The deeper inside yourself you go, the more in contact you are with yourself, with your partner, with the flow.

•Love can be felt and expressed spiritually or physically: One does not rule out the other. Instead of a machinelike preoccupation with foreplay and climax, love-making can become a graceful, ecstatic, and even sacred merging.

LOVE VS. LUST

•Love is the foundation for sex, not sex the foundation for love. The sexual drive, in its deepest and most profound sense, has the force of universal love behind it. The sex drive seeks not just sensory gratification but union.

•Sex "ups the ante" in the early phases of a relationship, making it more likely to prematurely become bonded, then later break up. Sexual pleasures may be so overshadowing that it becomes difficult to discern whether you really like each other or get along!

•Relationships built on the premise, "He who loves lust, loves best," are on very shaky ground. A sky-rocket romance may soon come crashing to earth. Sensate love by itself cannot last.

•A compulsive search for bigger and better orgasms can only produce flashes of excitement followed by periods of irritation. Sex not deepened by love soon becomes shallow and boring.

•The answer lies not in a return to sexual repression, but in developing our potential for love. As we grow in consciousness, sex becomes more than a game but a sacrament; love more than a fleeting emotion but the highest energy of all.

SEXUAL HEALTH

- In a healthy relationship love and sex become merged. While novelty may make a sexual partner enticing, sexual pleasures reach their most electrifying and consummate state in a deepening relationship.

- In such a context, sexual satisfaction and orgasm become enormously pleasurable, sometimes reaching ecstatic or mystical heights. Yet the absence of sexual relations is easily tolerated. There is no sexual addiction.

- Comparison with other partners or with a "better" night is the enemy of sexual enjoyment. Comparing is a cortical process while sexual pleasures are primarily subcortical. Tune in to the sensations of the moment, and whatever happens will more than suffice.

- Take responsibility for the pleasure of your own body, including orgasm. Get to know your sexuality; show your partner what turns you on. The more you know your own body, the more you'll have to share.

- Whatever you find yourselves doing in the flow of sexual love is right and beautiful. There can be much pleasure in being passively used, in giving service, in vigorously rubbing, squeezing, or biting. Wrestle, lick, suck even to the point of pain—as long as it is kept within mutually acceptable limits. Try a vibrator for added pleasure.

- You may want to take a voluntary break every once in a while, celibacy by your mutual consent. It can be a real turn-on! Your desires and attraction build up anew. Otherwise, if we repetitively experience sexual pleasures, we may become satiated and bored. Opt for highest quality not just quantity.

- In the healthy, animal instincts and sublime feelings, wild fantasies and tender considerations become synthesized and integrated.

SEXUAL DYSFUNCTION

•Sexual functioning requires a relatively rested and relaxed state of mind and body. When a person becomes anxious or tense, the biological capacity for sexual arousal becomes inhibited. This may result in impotence, premature ejaculation, or orgasmic dysfunction.

•"Sex is a natural function. There is no way we can teach a man to have an erection . . . or a woman to respond sexually. . . . We don't need to teach anything; we only need to remove the stumbling blocks," points out Dr. William Masters,‡ internationally known sex therapist.

•If you are receptive and are capable of responding to other people with empathy, warmth, and trust, if you enjoy the sensations of your body without any fear or guilt, then healthy and rewarding sexuality will generally come naturally and automatically. Healthy personality characteristics free of negative conditioning almost preclude sexual difficulties.

•Temporary bouts of sexual dysfunction resulting from fatigue, worries, overeating, or a recent emotional loss, are common. These generally go away on their own. Some ebb and flow in sexual responsiveness is natural.

•To enjoy sexual pleasures to a maximum remember some simple life habits: Stay well rested, eat lightly, drink in moderation,

‡ Address given to 1975 American Psychiatric Association Convention in Anaheim, California.

practice good bodily hygiene, exercise regularly, and above all else, stay vibrant and relaxed.

•More serious sexual difficulties may arise as a result of deeply ingrained negative feelings—guilt, shame, or anger—that stifle not just sexuality but the entire personality.

•If gripped by concern about performance, a man or a woman inhibits spontaneous abandonment to the natural flow of sexual experience. Such fear of performance causes muscular tension, emotional insensitivity, and a spectatorlike role, all of which reduce sexual responsiveness.

•Some people turn to alcohol in an attempt to cope with fear and other negative states. A small amount of alcohol may temporarily reduce anxiety, but overall, alcohol has a depressant effect upon sexuality. Chronic alcohol abuse may lead to impotence or orgasmic incompetence. Any cure in such cases must involve alcoholic abstention.

•Another small but significant cause of sexual dysfunction is organic impairment. Some of the typical illnesses that can disrupt sexual functioning are diabetes, multiple sclerosis, and thyroid dysfunction. A thorough medical exam is essential prior to any sex counseling.

•A sexual difficulty is an invitation to reevaluate what is going on in your life, physically, emotionally, spiritually, and in your relationships. Facing the roots of your problem may be initially discouraging, but honest self-appraisal is usually the biggest hurdle in solving a sexual difficulty.

•Masters and Johnson-trained sex therapists generally treat cases of sexual dysfunction by reducing anxiety and performance fears, and through graded sexual assignments. This systematic approach to the relearning of sexual abandon often has excellent results. For more information see your doctor.

SEXUAL FANTASY

•Sexual fantasies of all sorts are normal, and should be enjoyed without shame. Too many millions suffer from harmless fantasies because of inhibitions, guilt, or doubt.

•Give yourself permission to have fantasies; if you have a willing partner act them out (except for those that are truly offensive, violent, or dangerous): touch, tongue, tickle. Silk, satin, lace. The kitchen table or the couch. A parked car, a country meadow. Whatever. Wherever.

•A couple can mutually dis-inhibit, unwind on all levels and experience all joys. Begin by describing to each other your sexual fantasies. As you lose your inhibitions, so will your partner.

•Begin to enrich your love life now. On the following page jot down your most erotic fantasies, in rich and luscious detail.

•After this X-rated page is completed you may not be able to loan your book to your boss, but you can share it with your husband/wife or lover! Tonight, tomorrow, find a right time and setting. Be gentle, especially if your fantasy involves others.

•Innovate, explore, imagine. Howl, scream, purr. Anything goes as long as love prevails. Feel what is happening, in-joy!

X-RATED, IN-JOY

MULTI-ORGASM FOR TWO

•Modern-day research is shedding new light on our sexual possibilities, known really since ancient times. Sex researchers over the last twenty years have (re)discovered that both sexes are apparently capable of multiple orgasms.

•The trick is not trying for multiple orgasms. Culturally, our sex is too goal- and performance-oriented already. Extended orgasms are the result of complete ease and relaxation. Don't seek a new sex trophy, cultivate the natural.

•The male can gain voluntary control over his ejaculatory impulse. He experiences contractions for two or three seconds immediately before his usual ejaculation. This is his cue to stop thrusting, slow down, and hyper-enjoy each sensation.

•The male experiences the complete feelings of orgasm but without ejaculation. He doesn't try not to ejaculate. He simply stops moving, breathes deeply, and goes with the flow. This technique is also helpful to those who suffer from premature ejaculation.

•A cooperative partner is essential. Both must be sensitive to each other's impending signs of orgasm. Describe what is happening. As you learn to stop, relax, and slowly restart, you'll both relish the excitement that is mounting.

•This technique has been popular throughout history among those couples desirous of sexual intimacy, but who wish to practice continence as a means of spiritual evolution. It is known as

Karezza among the Hindus and ejaculatory control to the Oneida, who found ejaculation unnecessary to enjoying the ecstasies of love-making. (A caution: Practicing this technique to excess without ejaculation can lead to prostatitis.)

•These partial orgasms can be enjoyed by both sexes as much as one per minute. There is no frustration, to the contrary, pleasure builds. Most people, of course, feel no such prohibition against ejaculation, and, after protracted love-making, give in to a grand finale.

•Multiple orgasm is nothing to be achieved or aimed for. Sometimes it happens and sometimes it doesn't. If ejaculation comes, beautiful, so be it. The point is to enjoy the flow of here-and-now energy; to stop rushing, enjoy the view.

•Protracted love-making is another example of autonomic control. Along with reducing high blood pressure and turning off migraine headaches, modern man has now gained control over his ejaculatory impulse. A baseline state of restful alertness is the key to mastering all.

•This technique should build sexual togetherness in a couple, not competition or keeping score. Again, no tension, no trying—this gets in the way, impedes the flow. Abandon is the high road to ecstasy and delight.

SPIRITUAL LOVE-MAKING

•Most of us turn to sex for release, pleasure, and intimacy. At its best, in a committed love relationship, sex can provide all these things . . . and more.

•Throughout nature energies come together to produce higher levels of evolution. The male and the female come together not just for reproduction but for a higher creative purpose—the evolution and celebration of consciousness.

•Our sexual energy is that same energy which permeates the entire universe. Used wisely it propels us toward beauty, truth, and our higher self. Sexual energy is divine energy, and should be revered as such.

•In love-making you can unwind, unfold to a higher consciousness that is in us all. Give and take no longer have meaning. You both become man, you both become woman. Bodies merge together, your consciousness becomes one.

•To be complete the spiritual and emotional must match the physical. In joining, interpenetrating each other, the deepest parts of your soul can be opened to one another. The ego is left behind. Joy, tears, and surrender unfold.

•Pelvic movements may be powerful, gentle, or may cease entirely. Orgasm may happen or it may not. It matters not, for there is a beautiful and all-consuming love.

TANTRA

•The ancient Tibetan practice of tantra makes sex not just a biological function, but a divine and sacred ritual. It is for soulmates in search of a supreme love experience, and not an exotic mechanical procedure.

•Tantra is for married or very intimate partners to practice, after meditation or just before retiring. The whole experience takes at least an hour; allow for total privacy and no sense of rushing.

•Begin with nude dialogue (see pages 140–41). Remaining nude, the partners then practice yoga exercises, not for sexual athleticism but to further the process of letting go. Afterward, massage and the subtle laying on of hands heighten still more a mutual surrender to pleasure.

•Sexual excitement builds up in waves and settles down; the slower the build-up the better. Sexual intercourse is enjoyed when abandonment, ease, and rapport are at a maximum. In the classic tantra position, the woman settles into the lap of her lover, each with arms encircling the other.

•Sexual movements in this position are subtle, spontaneous, and from the inside. There is no urgency to orgasm while union is still maintained, so the couple is able to enjoy a most exquisite intimacy. But, please, comfort is essential, so any position of sexual intercourse can be enjoyed.

•Orgasm does not result from genital friction, but an involuntary reflex of total body involvement. Each partner can experience fully the orgasm of the other. Every atom of the body is overwhelmed with ecstasy, rapture, and grandeur. Ejaculation may or may not be desired.

CONCEIVED AND RECEIVED WITH LOVE

•A child should be a product of the fullness of love, not conceived to solve an unhappy marriage. The children we have deserve to be looked forward to, preferably with open arms.

•The first child, in particular, will require the most major adjustment of the young parents' lives, even more of a change than going from single to married. A totally dependent creature is about to arrive.

•A major responsibility you have to yourself and your child is to maximize your happiness and well-being. Children are a joy for sure, but also an enduring commitment. A fulfilled parent can more lovingly meet the needs of his child.

•Optimally, a pregnant woman ought to feel secure with herself and her marriage. If she feels insecure or afraid—feels unloved—her anxieties will be transmitted to her fetus. The fetus receives powerful imprints to its developing nervous system, via the bloodstream, muscular contractions, and even the sound of its mother's voice.

•At gestation's end, head first, the about-to-be-born is suddenly thrust down the birth canal; his nirvana shattered by pain, blood, and trauma. After such an arduous journey, let's greet the newborn properly, with a real and joyous celebration, not a mechanized hospital procedure.

•That's your child being born, not the obstetrician's. Consider natural childbirth. It's beautiful and forms a powerful bond between parents and child. Find a hospital that will allow the father into the delivery room, and the newborn to lie in with the mother.

LOVE: THE ESSENTIAL NUTRITION

•Numerous systems of infant care start from the assumption that if a baby receives a certain modicum of carbohydrate, fat, protein, vitamins and minerals, if he is kept warm and his bottom dry, then all will be well and good. But there is more to infant nurturing than feeding, diapering, and, in addition, "loving" it three or four times a day.

•Babies physically well nurtured but not properly loved may stop growing, waste away, and die. Love is not only an emotional need but critical to survival.

•At the turn of the century, almost every infant that was hospitalized under two years of age, died despite adequate feeding. The few survivors exhibited stunted growth and bizarre behavior. The cause of this disease was unknown until many years later: marasmus, caused by a lack of love. Is it any wonder that children with a deficiency of love grow up sickly, neurotic, or anti-social.

•An infant requires a steady modicum of love for optimal growth and development. Motherly love is essential for the infant to develop a firm foundation for inner security, trust that the world will meet its needs. Fathers, too, must participate in providing this motherly love, as can significant others.

•Breast-feeding that is mutual, personal, enjoyable, and reciprocal is a superb medium for psychological as well as biological growth in the first year of life. The infant is dominated by a need to retain mother, a need which when thwarted produces terror.

What greater intimacy than to be gently and securely held, hold mother's breast, suck her milk, and be lulled by her soft voice and heartbeat.

•We communicate our love to the infant primarily through our fingers. A baby can greatly benefit from being stroked and massaged, for about fifteen minutes four times daily. Stroke in a head-to-foot progression, concentrating on the head. After each session, rock and cuddle your baby for another five minutes. The quality of tactile stimulation can have a lasting effect upon an infant's growth and development.

FREUD WAS RIGHT

•Freud was right. Childhood experience is crucial in determining the future personality. While coping with frustration is a necessary lesson of later life, need gratification is the precursor of health. Maternal rejection can give rise to a whole range of disorders, psychological and physical.

•Eczema, asthma, or ulcers may result if a child is deprived of an adequate amount of love. Frustration resulting from a lack of love may be turned inward into a chronic depressive cast or outward into aggressive acts.

•Shoplifting is an example, sometimes traceable to maternal deprivation. Shoplifting is often done compulsively, by people financially well off. The stealing has little to do with money but a striving for that which is unconsciously lacking: mother's love. Macy's and Gimbel's have become displaced mothers.

•The search for power, prestige, and admiration may be another means of seeking mother's—the world's—approval. Paradoxically, hyperachievement, just like anti-social behavior, may be an unconscious means of gaining the attention desperately missing from childhood.

•Children are hurt deeply when their mother or father ignores them but unduly praise other children. This is often the beginning of an inferiority complex and self-hatred. Treat your children with real respect, never with humiliation. They are fellow human beings in the process of unfolding.

•Attitudes toward one's children become self-fulfilling. If you, a priori, see your child as beautiful or a nuisance, it frequently will become just that. Attitudes toward one's children are partially derived from earlier love felt for father, mother, brother, or sister, or a disowned part of self.

•How well a human being develops his capacities for love, happiness, and productivity will depend upon the training he receives in childhood. "Training"—not just on the toilet or in the school—but from all significant others. Fathers and mothers are the key, but we all collectively raise our next generation.

•Children are a mirror of their emotional environment. Surrounded with love, they mostly are joyful; amid tension they become "impossible." Children do not develop properly under the stormy skies of a discordant marriage. Look to the health of your marriage.

•If parents practice meditation, they will have more energy for their children; less stress, more love will pervade the home. In addition, Parent Effectiveness Training (P.E.T.) is recommended to help maximize parenting skills.

TOO MUCH LOVE?

•Parents can never love a child too much or too well. You needn't fear spoiling a child by making him too happy. The happiness you nurture kindles all future affections and fulfillment.

•Never leave a baby in the first year alone to cry. He may be hungry, cold, hot, wet, etc.—or may simply need love, reassurance, and contact. Such attentiveness instills a basic attitude of trust and safety—"Mother is at home, everything is going to be okay"—which provides confidence and security the whole life through.

•Children require powerful expressions of affection, including nursing, touching, holding, tactile and visual exploration. The caressing a child receives from mother and father plays a crucial role in his development of friendships, and all future love relations. Comfortableness with play and conversation, become later derivatives of "touching," making contact.

•Children need your service. It's just that simple. That's why nature equipped them with a loud cry, so their needs could be heard. No child ever suffered from being loved too much or too often, if the quality of love is right.

•Love your child as unconditionally as possible. So what if it splatters some milk. Develop your internal stability and it will help negate any emotional upset. The kitchen floor can be easily cleaned; the child can learn optimally without being yelled at.

•Unconditional love instills confidence in natural behavior. The child doesn't grow up afraid he'll be "found out" as someone bad, to be discarded. Nor does he grow up compulsively striving to win a measure of fleeting acceptance. Unconditional love allays all fears. The child properly loved grows up fearless.

•That is not to say that discipline or boundary setting are not necessary or important. They are. But firmness can be shared in a loving fashion. It is not an excuse for hostility.

THE CHILDREN OF TOMORROW

•The most beautiful words of advice on parenting come from Kahlil Gibran*:

Your children are not your children
They are the sons and daughters of life's longing for itself.
They come through you but not from you,
And though they are with you yet they belong not to you.

You may give them your love but not your thoughts,
For they have their own thoughts.
You may house their bodies but not their souls.
For their souls dwell in the house of tomorrow, which you cannot visit, not even in your dreams.
You may strive to be like them but seek not to make them like you.
For life goes not backward nor tarries with yesterday.

You are the bows from which your children as living arrows are sent forth.
The archer sees the mark upon the path of the infinite, and He bends you with His might that His arrows may go swift and far.
Let your bending in the archer's hand be for gladness;
For even as He loves the arrow that flies,
So He loves also the bow that is stable.

* Kahlil Gibran, *The Prophet*. Alfred A. Knopf, New York, 1976, pp. 17–18.

YOUR FAMILY ROOTS

•Remember your parents saying, "You'll never understand what it's like to be a parent until you're one yourself." Everything comes full circle in life. When first we become a parent, then we experience the gratitude of being a child.

•Adolescent turmoil and rebellion sometimes lead to a shattering of parental ties. As the noise settles down, rekindle the relationship. Make peace with your parents. In so doing, you make peace with yourself.

•Speak to your family elders. Have them tell you of their parents, childhood, customs, and times. You'll gain a deepening appreciation of your history and tradition, your roots.

•Have a family reunion. Yep, even if your Aunt Agnes is a little flaky and you can't stand your Cousin Morris. In this age of families being spread all over the world, there is great power and love in a gathering of the clan.

•Our "blood relatives" are for shared devotion, responsibility and caring—not to limit our love for the "stranger." Our family doesn't end with our second cousins. We are all part of the family of man.

TRANSCENDING

–The Transcendent
–Gateway to Love
–Love Consciousness
–Guiding Light
–Spirituality
–Are You a Mystic?
–Spiritual Crises
–Faith
–Put Love First
–The Power of Prayer
–Life After Death?
–Higher Consciousness
–Toward an Enlightened You
–Integration of Opposites
–Universal Values
–Truth
–The Imprisoned Splendor
–Creativity
–Beauty
–Nature
–A Million, Million Miracles
–Save Our Planet
–Wisdom
–A Loving Education
–Devotion
–Service
–Brotherly Love
–Justice
–Joyous Simplicity
–Imagine!
–A Realized Society
–It Could All Begin with You
–Toward a New Age
–Transformation at the Speed of Love

THE TRANSCENDENT

•Inherent in growing, sharing, in the very structure of love and life itself, is transcending, going beyond ourselves. The transcendent is the source of all time, space, and causality. It is the field of eternal love, unboundedness, infinite, pure intelligence, permeating all.

•Though the transcendent is not immediately obvious, it underlies all strata of creation. You are the transcendent, I am the transcendent, all of creation is the transcendent—in its most essential nature.

•In our scientific age the transcendent is no longer being thought of as occult or esoteric; on the contrary, it is being demonstrated to be of real and lasting value. Knowledge of the transcendent can help you to live the fullest values of life; enrich the love of your life beyond your wildest dreams.

•The need to transcend, to go beyond the limits of our ego, the confines of our personality, may be a need in the same sense that we need vitamins and carbohydrates: If the need is not filled, we become ill and dissatisfied.

•A mature love relationship is a beautiful, satisfying means of ego transcendence. In transcending we break free from the narrow boundaries of our existence to the unitive force which underlies all.

Thou transcendent,
Nameless, the fibre and the breath,
Light of the light, shedding forth universes, thou
centre of them,

Thou mightier centre of the true, the good, the loving,
Thou moral, spiritual fountain—affection's source—
thou reservoir,
Thou pulse—thou motive of the stars, suns, systems
That, circling, move in order, safe, harmonious,
Athwart the shapeless vastnesses of space,
How should I think, how breathe a single breath,
how speak, if, out of myself,
I could not launch, to those, superior universes?

Walt Whitman
"Passage to India,"
Leaves of Grass

GATEWAY TO LOVE

•The transcendent: Shakespeare, Balzac, Emerson, and Whitman lauded it; Socrates, Plato, Spinoza, and Kant gave it philosophical expression; Newton, Kepler, Einstein, and Schrödinger described its physical imprint: Moses, Christ, Krishna, and Buddha summoned us to its glory.

•Almost every religion teaches that the kingdom of heaven lies within; that to realize its glory is man's highest priority: "First seek ye the kingdom of heaven and all else will be added unto thee." So begin to look inward wherein lies the kingdom of heaven, a rich source of blessings worldly and divine.

•A simple meditation technique, TM, makes the transcendental experience universally available. Diving deep into the unbounded ocean of love within, meditation expands our hearts and inspires us to be more loving. Just as a light bulb spreads light everywhere by virtue of being lit, we begin spontaneously to spread more love and harmony.

•The transcendent is our gateway to love.

Love	Unbounded
Joy	Infinite
Intelligence	Immortal

Different words for the ecstatic experience open to each of us of universality.

LOVE CONSCIOUSNESS

•Love is differently perceived from different levels of consciousness. On the physical level, love is an emotion, but in its purest state love is an energy or radiation that pervades the whole cosmos (it is the life-supporting energy which underlies all creation).

•Love takes us from the pangs of separation to the joy of eternal union. With age and experience love is meant to grow in fulfillment. It grows in toys and playfields, in friendships and in marriage. As love overflows it becomes a way of being, an attitude, a relatedness to all of life.

•As the magnitude of our heart expands, our love gains the status of an ocean, unfathomable and full. All-embracing and unshakable, the fullness of our love shines through amid the ever-changing circumstances of time.

• Outer acts are the result of our inner attitudes. As consciousness is suffused with love, our thoughts naturally become more life-supporting. Actions become powerful and compassionate, generating more waves of fulfillment for all.

•What we who pass so swiftly experience as songs, pleasures, or cries of pain are only overtones in a very much larger harmony. Love, our contact with that larger and more universal harmony, expands our appreciation and understanding.

•Love *is;* whatever enters the stream of our awareness is loved. Everything becomes a reflection of that love, no matter how misdirected or peculiar a particular manifestation. Soon, love permeates all.

GUIDING LIGHT

•Love is the sweet force of life, powerful yet sublime. He who loves is aware of the universal love working through him. Personal love is focused universal love: As our intimate relations deepen, so does our universal appreciation.

•The guiding principle of creation is love. All diversity, all manifestations of existence are infused with an underlying unity. At every stage of universal and personal evolution, love is there to guide the way.

•There shimmers within us a light, the light of love eternal. Let it be your guide. As your heart opens, you'll become more sensitive but also strong. Wrong action will make you weak, and right action powerful. But whether you initially go slow or fast, know that love will lead you toward fulfillment.

•Love makes acorns into mighty oak trees, amoebas (eventually) into you and me. Nature organizes supremely, with wisdom and economy. Let go, trust in the universal flow.

•Just as love is essential for the proper growth and development of the human organism, so love is essential for the growth and development of our human race collectively. We are all part of a larger and wiser life-organism. Feel this higher intelligence in the softest murmurings of your heart, then bring forth its noblest intentions.

SPIRITUALITY

•Spiritual refers to the experience of wholeness and integration. The whole of life is greater than the sum of its parts. Spirituality refers to that something extra which results from a fully integrated heart and mind.

•Life seeks to complete itself and become whole in all its manifestations. Life desires more, maximum love, maximum achievement, maximum joy, until it gains fulfillment. This evolutionary force, this ever "more" is spirit.

•With the growth of spirituality, the wholeness gets reflected: We see life as an indivisible whole. The smallest happening, everything, derives infinite significance from a higher, more universal order. As this higher order becomes more strongly felt, the result is a superior happiness and serenity of soul.

•Love is the divine spirit in man. "Thou are That," say the Upanishads, the absolute, loving spirit of the world. While we live on earth, we can breathe the immortal, and in the process live love incarnate.

•There is today a rising spirituality, sometimes imperceptible, but becoming increasingly more evident. A spiritual emergence with respect for the sacredness of every person and culture; growth toward world unity and harmony. The false dichotomies are melting away within man, between man and his neighbor, and man and all creation. A time for rebirth, a new cosmology, is at hand.

ARE YOU A MYSTIC?

•Surveys suggest that today at least 40 per cent of American adults are having spiritual experiences. "The feeling of being very close to a powerful spiritual force that seemed to lift you out of yourself."† Are you one of our emerging nation of mystics?

•People of all ages, races, nationalities, and occupations report a virtually identical experience of ecstasy, of rebirth, of knowing the "way things really are." This experience of "absolute" knowledge gives the person an unshakable conviction and profound understanding of life's basic goodness and unity, and leaves him totally comfortable with his place in the larger scheme of things.

•The awakening is accompanied by an overwhelming feeling of happiness, an ecstatic joy that fills the person with a deep sense of peace, love, and understanding. All who have had it are significantly changed, never to be quite the same.

•In a spiritual awakening, the glory of the transcendent shines through. The greater part of the best in philosophy, religion, science, and the arts come from those who have awakened (Plato, Christ, Newton, Shakespeare, just to name a few).

•The combined testimony from today's solid, upstanding middle-American "mystics," along with our history's most realized souls, builds a powerful case for the transcendent. Perhaps as you read the great sages, saints, and seers, a voice deep inside of you whispers, "Yes, it is so."

† Andrew M. Greeley and William C. McCready, "Are We a Nation of Mystics?" New York *Times Magazine*, January 26, 1975.

SPIRITUAL CRISES

- Spiritual awakenings are profound and ecstatic, but they may also be alarming or disruptive. For fear of being thought "crazy," most never speak of them to anyone.

- Many healthy and stable individuals have mystical experiences, which may cause them to feel initially unsettled or confused. It is important to see such an experience as a breakthrough, a progression, rather than as a regression, escape, or a mini-psychotic episode.

- An ecstatic state may last for moments, hours, or even days, but it is bound to cease. When the knowingness and experience of life's oneness, love, and joy begin to fade, a personal crisis may ensue. The person may believe, falsely, he has fallen lower than he was before.

- Another kind of spiritual crisis, seen mostly in those over thirty, may be due to a lack of experience of life's deeper reality. Despite worldly successes, the person experiences a sense of growing boredom, emptiness, and sterility, "something missing." He may be living at the apparent zenith of health and prosperity when this progressive inner disturbance catches him by surprise.

- The key to overcoming a spiritual crisis is first to recognize the cause. If it is protracted, support and understanding from a proper spiritual guide can be helpful. Passages from Christ, Buddha, Maharishi, Wordsworth, or Blake can help validate the universality of the experience.

- A temporary experience of the transcendent may act like a window, helping the person get on the path to total enlightenment. A person in crisis might consider growth-oriented psychotherapy, learning meditation, and strengthening any previous religious tie or outlook.

FAITH

•The heights of humility, virtue, tenderness, and courage have been won through religious service. A soul who has gained grace is capable of the highest nobility mankind has ever known.

•Love is the foundation of the Christian religion and is extolled and glorified by every spiritual discipline. Whether by prayer or confession, piety or great charity, for the fruits of service to God to be realized, love and humility must reign. Love at its deepest level is the religious impulse, spirit seeking to recognize and reunite with itself.

•Faith comes not by straining or stringent trying. One must relax, fall back on the larger power. The divine which you are seeking has been welling up in your own being; seek it out. Yield, and God will do the rest.

•Faith enlarges life. Personal motives and desires are small in comparison to religious exaltation. Fears and anxieties melt away; serenity fills the soul. Courage and fortitude become mainstays through good times and bad.

•The key to faith is surrender to a higher power than ourselves. A secondhand faith of mere convention and dull habit does little for the soul. True religious life is a passion full of wonder, enthusiasm, and experience of the divine.

•There is a universal desire, which underlies all religious life, and that is to transcend. The lifeblood of religious genius is experience of the divine. Capture the transcendent and all isms lead to God.

•Faith can be giving oneself over to God or be of a more secular kind. A measure of transcendence can be gained through devoting oneself to a great ideal or patriotic cause.

•You can get to know the personality of God by opening yourself up to him/her directly, or by loving others and the creation (getting to know the artist through his works).

•Belief underlies everything in this world. If you plant a seed, water it, then return to see it grow, you have trust in a higher order. No merchant would make wares if he didn't have trust in his market. How much more faith is it, really, to love and trust the Lord.

•The most profound service we can do God is doing for His other children. Be of good cheer, aid the weak, render good amid evil, honor all. Religion is not just to be judged by words and feelings but the quality of our lives.

•Religion doesn't have to be an austere and somber matter; worship need not be with a furrowed brow. Religion, rather, can be a grateful admiration, a rejoicing in existence.

•The rising spirituality we are witnessing is not so much a "belief," a conception in the intellect. Rather, it is an extension of consciousness in which we come to feel God. We have an experience of harmony, an intimation of the divine.

PUT LOVE FIRST

I may speak in tongues of men or of angels, but if I am without love, I am a sounding gong or a clanging cymbal. I may have the gift of prophecy, and know every hidden truth; I may have faith strong enough to move mountains; but if I have not love, I am nothing. I may dole out all I possess, or even give my body to be burnt, but if I have no love, I am none the better.

Love is patient; love is kind and envies no one. Love is never boastful, nor conceited, nor rude; never selfish, not quick to take offense. Love keeps no score of wrongs; does not gloat over other men's sins, but delights in the truth. There is nothing love cannot face; there is no limit to its faith, its hope, and its endurance.

Love will never come to an end. Are there prophets? Their work will be over. Are there tongues of ecstasy? They will cease. Is there knowledge? It will vanish away; for our knowledge and our prophecy alike are partial, and the partial vanishes when wholeness comes. When I was a child, my speech, my outlook, and my thoughts were all childish. When I grew up, I had finished with childish things. Now we see only puzzling reflections in a mirror, but then we shall see face to face. My knowledge now is partial; then it will be whole, like God's knowledge of me. In a word, there are three things that last forever: Faith, Hope, and Love; but the greatest of them all is love.

Put love first.

—St. Paul
1 Corinthians 13
The New English Bible
1970, p. 221

THE POWER OF PRAYER

•All is possible for the humble and contrite heart, so let your silent voice rise to God like a river returning to its ocean. Prayer is any kind of inward communion or dialogue with that which you recognize as divine.

•Too many people regard prayer as a ritualized repetition of words, childish petition for gain, or even a sign of weakness. When the soul is pure prayer can accomplish great things.

•Mature prayer can produce an increase in grace, absorption, and power. In the process of prayerful communion, energy—from on high—is mobilized. The living God becomes a reality again, the eternal is reawakened.

•A phenomenon gaining increasing scientific recognition is that prayers by and for the sick can contribute to recovery. As a doctor, I have seen patients, after all other therapy has failed, cured of despair and ill health by the serene effort of prayer.

•Cultivate a general stance of gratitude. As St. Francis in his divine innocence taught, let us offer praise for brother sun and sister moon, for diverse fruits and flowers.

•Grace before meals is a beautiful habit for you and your family to consider. A formal thanksgiving can be offered or else for a few moments done by each person in silence. Perhaps hold hands around the table, as you draw from your spiritual center. Done sincerely, mealtimes become more of a high and loving vibration.

LIFE AFTER DEATH?

•With the dawn of transcendental consciousness there is no longer a fear of dying. Death is recognized by those who awaken, as a shift in modes of life or consciousness, a transition. Physical death is a passing incident, with continued evolution of our individuality.

•Modern investigation,‡ using accounts of patients who have died and come back, suggests what we have been taught for two thousand years—the existence of life after death.

•The similarity among various reports is striking. The patient may hear himself pronounced dead by his doctor. All have experienced floating out of their physical bodies, then moving very rapidly through a long dark tunnel.

•The "dead" patient may see his own body, even watch his resuscitation as though he were a spectator. As the initial shock wears off and he becomes more comfortable, he notices he has a new "spiritual body," made of light but invisible to others.

•Soon he is greeted by loved ones of his who have previously died, to help him in his transition. Also, he feels drawn to a loving, warm spirit, a being of indescribable brilliance and light; some might see in this light the Christ, Buddha, or an angel, depending on their religious orientation.

‡ Elizabeth Kubler-Ross, *On Death and Dying*. Macmillan Co., New York, 1969. Raymond Moody, *Life After Life*. Bantam Books, New York, 1975.

- He is then shown a panoramic, instantaneous playback of the events of his life, and asked to evaluate what lessons he has learned. He is being made ready for the next life. Just then he finds he must go back, his time has not yet come.

- Peace, love, joy, and wholeness suffuse the person throughout his out-of-body experience. So intense is the bliss that a seemingly universal experience is of not wanting to come back. Post-resuscitation, life is forever changed. He knows beyond a doubt, there is life after death.

HIGHER CONSCIOUSNESS

•Let's not wait until death or dying, a hereafter, to gain transcendental treasures. Let's have it happen now. The transcendent lies deep within you, a limitless source of bliss, intelligence, and power.

•All religions describe it and seek to attain it—cosmic consciousness, nirvana, liberation, moksha, or samadhi. Call it what you will. The shift is to an entirely new frame, a higher state of consciousness.

•Moses, Christ, St. Paul, Krishna, Shankara, Buddha, Lao-tzu, and Mohammed—our greatest spiritual leaders—all point in the same direction, toward the same cosmic end. The individual merges in oneness with the Absolute; spiritual resolution is achieved.

•While the human potential for achieving higher states of consciousness has been recognized for centuries, the possibility has remained obscure. Recently, however, science has begun to investigate the neurophysiology of enlightenment.*

•Higher consciousness can apparently be cultivated through a systematic development and integration of our body, mind, and spirit. Far from a state of self-delusion or self-denial, enlightenment represents a very practical state of our full human potential.

* Harold H. Bloomfield and Robert Kory, *Happiness: The TM Program, Psychiatry, and Enlightenment*. Simon & Schuster, New York, 1976.

TOWARD AN ENLIGHTENED YOU

•What are the characteristics of the enlightened individual? Is it possible to pick him or her out of a crowd? Does he walk on water, perform other supernatural feats?

•While the enlightened individual does have some remarkable characteristics, at the same time, he appears quite normal and natural. What could be more normal than functioning at your full potential? Let's review some of these characteristics, for the state of enlightenment being your birthright, these can be yours before too long.

•Happiness becomes a baseline experience, complete and unconditional. He is saturated with a supreme awe and wonder for the cosmos and its splendor.

•A natural innocence characterizes his interactions with others. Against a background of mature emotional and intellectual development, bubbles a childlike spontaneity. As a result, good humor and laughter are his constant companions.

•He experiences love at the sight, taste, smell, sound, or touch of everything. His love is unbounded and universal, impartially flowing in all directions. Personal love and intimacy grow deeply, without any fears or inhibition.

•His unshakable inner contentment insures a permanent state of freedom. He is free from unconscious cravings or unfulfilled desires, which distort accurate thinking and perception. The windows of perception are cleansed; he perceives life's glory.

•Established in the transcendent he comes in tune with cosmic purpose. Every thought, word, and action becomes spontaneously right and life-supporting.

•His intellect is clear and lucid, capable of the deepest penetration. He can maintain broad comprehension of a situation while focusing sharply on its details. He entertains all possibilities, turning obstacles into opportunities.

•He embodies skill in action; actions are easy, orderly, and purposeful. He goes straight to the target, to bring maximum good effect to others and himself.

•He is unique, a non-conformist, yet steeped in traditional values, universal. Enlightenment does not homogenize; on the contrary, individuality blossoms. But at bottom he knows himself to be what we all truly are: omniscient, immortal, beyond pleasure-pain, eternal.

INTEGRATION OF OPPOSITES

•Experience of the transcendent can apparently harmonize the polarities of human existence. Our rational-analytic and creative-intuitive modes of consciousness become more synchronous and better integrated. The scientist and the artist, the pragmatist and the dreamer, receive nourishment and insight from transcendental experience.

•Another conflict bridged by the transcendent is that of reason and emotion. The infusion of wholeness acts to harmonize thoughts and feelings, our "will" and our "want." Compulsions and cravings lose their power; we mature more rapidly.

•The transcendental silence integrates another age-old polarity, that of the spirit and the flesh. The spiritual and the physical dimensions of personality become strengthened, and soon their interdependence becomes recognized. Reverence and playfulness, responsibility and pleasure cease to be antagonistic. These become complementary in their emerging wholeness.

•The growth of wholeness integrates any apparent conflict between the needs of self and others. As a person transcends the boundaries and concerns of the small self, he experiences transcendental fullness. Dissolved are the fears and insecurities which fuel any narrow-minded selfishness. Joyful and self-sufficient, he now extends the full value of himself to others.

•There are, of course, many other polarities—stability/flexibility, tradition/innovation, independence/dependence, and so on. Too much one-sided development of any of these forces can eventually produce conflict and suffering. For a harmonious existence, we need the integrative quality of the transcendent.

UNIVERSAL VALUES

•We human beings sometimes cling to insecurities, falsehood or manipulation—for fear of letting go, opening up to a higher freedom and power. But there comes a time when we must leave these lesser value, to favor our higher self.

•The crossing may have its difficulties, we may experience some void, some loss for a time, but these are small compared to the higher values and richness of pleasure of experiencing life more deeply.

•Virtue can never be produced by the imposition of authority. Conformity, yes, but not virtue; virtue must come from within. Forcing upon the individual an externally formulated code of behavior often leads to rebellion, stunted growth, or doubt.

•The transition to an awakened consciousness must be from within. The enlightened person no longer has "moral problems," in the usual sense. He automatically computes his action from a broader perspective. He is permanently identified with the larger good.

•Higher values give impetus to transcending; their growth leads to an all-encompassing perspective. Just as water may be an ocean in one place, a river in another, so truth, creativity, beauty, wisdom, devotion, service, and justice are different expressions of one another, and the same universal core.

TRUTH

•Truthfulness is the fountainhead of all personal excellence. Established in the ever-constant, never-changing truth of the transcendent, your every action becomes precise. Live by truth and you will pay truth its greatest honor.

•The least taint of a lie, any attempt to make a good impression, and vanity will mar the result. But speak truth and nature bears you witness; everything becomes more fresh and alive.

•Deceit and manipulation notwithstanding, the larger truth survives all shams. Truth is invincible, it does not require being rigidly adhered to or a stoic defense. Just keep your mind receptive, cultivate inner silence, and the truth will naturally shine through.

•The artist and the scientist both point the way to higher truth. The scientist seeks truth in each small observation, whether he beholds a subatomic particle or a galaxy of stars. The artist unveils truth with his every brush stroke or with his nuance of word. Both roads lead to infinity and bring us to the transcendent's door.

•Enlightenment awakens inner truth, knowledge of ourselves. He who lives the fullness of life's glory can speak it out, and raise a glimmer, a call to truth in those about him. More is gained planting a noble truth in the heart of your neighbor than flattering your ego before thousands.

THE IMPRISONED SPLENDOR

Truth is within ourselves; it takes no rise
From our outward things, whatever you may believe;
There is an inmost center in us all,
Where truth abides in fullness; and around,
Wall within wall, the gross flesh hems it in,
Perfect and true perception—which is truth;
A baffling and perverting carnal mesh
Which blinds it, and makes error; and "to know"
Rather consists in opening out a way
Whence the imprison'd splendor may dart forth,
Than in effecting entry for the light
Supposed to be without.

—Robert Browning
Paracelsus

CREATIVITY

•The nature of existence is to continually create new expressions and forms. Marvel at the diversification present within you, about you, and in all of creation. Your creative urge is part of the larger flow. The trick to its full expression lies in the integration of your body, mind, and spirit.

•The human creative act is a multi-step operation, originating in the mind. The inspiration seems to come from on high, a thought that germinates unconsciously, the "aha" reponse, a light that flickers on. This newfound gift must then be lent energy and dynamism to assure its proper fruition. We must plan, design, build, and refine.

•The left hemisphere of the brain specializes in rational, analytic abilities; it is our intellectual side. The right or silent hemisphere specializes in intuitive, holistic abilities; it is our artistic side. For maximum creativity we must integrate both our brain hemispheres lest we be one-sided.

•The great creatives among us are also the most humble, for they can feel inspiration coming from a more universal source than their personal ego. The source of creativity is the transcendent. By attunement to the transcendent we can maximize our creative expression.

•A new discovery depends not just on innovative thinking, but immersing yourself in a time-tested tradition of knowledge. As Sir Isaac Newton stated, "If I have seen further than most men, it is because I have stood on the shoulders of giants." Creativity builds upon tradition in giving rise to progress.

•An enduring creative act is like a drop in which you can locate the ocean. A work that is to be coveted through the millennia does not just bear the stamp of its time, but a lasting imprint from the transcendent.

•You needn't be a superstar; creativity has its own rewards. Take the guitar lessons you've been putting off, mold pottery, or write poetry; it's not very hard.

•Love is creative. It unfolds the potentialities of lover as well as beloved. The sensitivity and attunement which love brings can transform every aspect of living into an art. Beauty, charm, and grace become the norm.

BEAUTY

•When you find beauty in some compartment of nature, in a combination of sounds, a pattern of colors, or well-proportioned shapes and forms, you are not merely marveling at some external object but are gaining a glimpse of the beauty which lies within you.

•The best part of beauty cannot be expressed by words, picture, or pose. Real beauty exists in the transcendent, apart from the object, however subtle. This beauty is potentially mirrored in every object, from electrons revolving around a nucleus to distant galaxies and beyond.

•The same qualities that go into making a painting or landscape beautiful go into making a "beautiful" person. Beauty is no accident; it is as orderly as gravity. Like faith and justice, it is but a different facet of the transcendental all.

•A stressed individual possesses a physiology and psychology that is disorderly and chaotic. As a result he may be critical of his surroundings and unappreciative of its beauty. Unless beauty is within us, we can travel the world over and find it not.

•To become a beautiful person, we must order the different parts of our life. Each part—spirit, mind, body, emotions, senses—must be strong and healthy, enriching and enhancing the others to create an over-all sense of harmony and wholeness.

•In the flow of our love, we are naturally in tune, and that which is naturally in tune is beautiful. Given the proper inner development we tend to do things tunefully, beautifully. As the *I Ching* says, "His beauty is within, but it gives freedom to his limbs and expresses itself in his works."

- We convey our inner state through our bodily movements. The garbage collector, the street sweeper, can accomplish their work routine in a beautiful and uplifting fashion. They needn't be ballet dancers. Grace of action, action that is pleasing, radiates inner beauty and love of life.

- Cultivate a habit of listening to great music. Music can soothe a troubled heart and refine your spirit. It can transport you from the material plane onto another. Great and beautiful music is the infinite made audible.

- As you grow in love, in higher consciousness, everything becomes more beautiful. Your attention is directed to life's rosebuds, not its thorns. A smile at the grocery store makes your shopping a delight. You have the perception of an artist: Beauty is yours.

NATURE

•Natural beauty is the highest beauty of all. No need to gild a lily or perfume a rose. Every creature, every living thing has its own intrinsic beauty (if not choked by rubbish or deadening air).

•Nurture silence in your soul and caterpillars will whisper to you their story, a field of dandelions becomes a cosmic dance, trees will wave to you, and a mouse becomes your friend.

•Commune with Mother Nature. Look at a scarlet tulip, drops of dew glistening on some leafy plant; the smell and feel of freshly turned earth. Relax, be with it, let yourself go. Soon your heart will swell to receive the love by which Mother Nature sustains us all.

•Nature has so much to teach. Pick up a fallen leaf. See its delicate veins, the perfection of its shape. Use it as a ten-foot mandala.

•Being with nature is not just a luxury, a vacation, but a necessity for right and balanced living. Take the advice of the great naturalist John Muir: "Climb the mountains and get their good tidings. Nature's peace will flow into you as sunshine flows into trees. The winds will flow their own freshness into you and the storms their energy, while cares will drop off like autumn leaves."

A MILLION, MILLION MIRACLES

•With the dawn of higher consciousness, a rose, a beach, each of us—becomes the most remarkable expression in the world. Love, nature, the transcendent—all intertwine in divine mystery, the million, million miracles of existence. We must awaken from our collective inertia to a new sense of awe.

•As our great seers have proclaimed:

To look at any thing,
If you would know that thing,
You must look at it long:
To look at this green and say
"I have seen spring in these
Woods," will not do—you must
Be the thing you see:
You must be the dark snakes of
Stems and ferny plumes of leaves,
You must enter in
To the small silences between
The leaves,
You must take your time
And touch the very peace
They issue from.

—John Moffitt

Love all God's creation, the whole and every
grain of sand in it. Love every leaf, every
ray of God's light. Love the animals, love the

plants, love everything. If you love everything you will perceive the divine mystery in things. Once you perceive it, you will begin to comprehend it better every day. And you will come at last to love the whole world with an all-embracing love.

—Fyodor Dostoyevsky

It is strange to talk of miracles, revelations, inspiration, and the like, as things past, while love remains.

—William Blake

Flower in the crannied wall,
I pluck you out of the crannies,
I hold you, root and all, in my hand,
Little flower—but *if* I could understand
What you are, root and all, and all in all,
I should know what God and man is.

—Alfred Lord Tennyson

Some skeptics say, "Oh, the miracles, I can't accept miracles." One may drop a brown seed in the black soil and up comes a green shoot. You let it grow and by and by you pull up its root and you find it red. You cut the red root and find it has a white heart. Can any one tell how this comes about—how brown cast into black results in green and then in red and white? Yet you eat your radish without troubling your mind over miracles. Men are not distressed by miracles in the dining room; they reserve them all for religion!

—William Jennings Bryan

The most beautiful thing we can experience is the mysterious. It is the source of all true art and science. He to whom this emotion is a stranger, who can no longer pause to wonder and stand rapt in awe, is as good as dead: his eyes are closed.

—Albert Einstein

SAVE OUR PLANET

• We are one with our environment. All living forms are synthesized into a huge interdependence upon our spaceship earth. We have been most unloving toward our planet, and now our sins are coming back to haunt us.

• Perhaps 90 per cent of cancers are caused by environmental pollutants, especially in industrialized nations. Progress at the cost of pollution has poisoned our food, water, and air.

• Ozone in our stratosphere absorbs much of the ultraviolet radiation from the sun. Fluorocarbons in aerosol sprays, nitrogen fertilizers, and now supersonic transports are reducing this precious ozone. If this process is left unchecked, the result could be far-reaching damage to the plant and animal life, climatic disasters, and a higher incidence of skin cancer.

• Coastal areas that support important fisheries are being destroyed or damaged by offshore oil drilling, reclamation, and dumping of industrial wastes.

• The soil available for raising crops is rapidly being eroded by lack of care, mismanagement, and overcultivation.

• We have heartlessly exterminated whole species of animals, such as the passenger pigeon and dodo bird. Think of it, a unique gift of creation destroyed forever. Whales, dolphins, porpoises, seals, crocodiles, and marine turtles are now endangered species. Many of your cosmetics, fur coats, and pocketbooks are being made from species threatened with extinction. Remember this next time you shop.

•We humans do not own or have exclusive right to the planet. We are only one of the earth's inhabitants. We share the skies with birds and butterflies, the seas with fish and fellow mammals, the land with animals, large and tiny, that climb, graze, and burrow.

•We have made a mess of the Garden of Eden we were entrusted with. Ozone, endangered species, carcinogenic agents, soil erosion, reforestation, the energy crisis, nuclear catastrophe —become familiar not only with these terms but the major issues these involve.

•To clean up and purify our planet, international cooperation on a scale not seen so far in history is essential. Work with the World Wildlife Fund, Sierra Club, and other such organizations. It's no longer just a matter of pride in our earthly home but even perhaps our survival.

WISDOM

•Wisdom is the ability to look beneath surface glitter to an object's intrinsic quality and true worth. The wise know true ends from false, and lofty things from low.

•All of life is good and right in its essential nature. Evil comes to be seen as the absence of knowledge and love. The way to eliminate ignorance and hatred is not through the endless analysis of their manifestations, but through introducing more love and understanding.

•We are all part of a huge teaching machine. At the point we learn "Thou art That," all the glories of the universe unfold. Intuitively or analytically, through the heart or through the intellect, higher knowledge is a resource available to us all.

•The wise know we belong to the transcendent even more intimately than we belong to the material world. Not only is the transcendent that from which we have come and toward which we are heading, but our contact with it produces noticeable effects in this world.

•When we commune with the transcendent, our finite personality becomes transformed. We gain a much greater measure of contentment, vision, and power. Our universe takes a turn for the better, or for the worse, to the degree we open ourselves to the transcendental divine.

•The wise know that not only they themselves but the whole universe of emerging beings are in most loving and orderly hands. Tragedy, dissolution, even death, are not the final end. Live by eternal wisdom and you will regain the paradise lost.

A LOVING EDUCATION

•The goal of education is to help each person become all that he is capable of becoming. Imparting skills and information is certainly essential, but so is developing a fully functioning, loving human being.

•A child raised lovingly will learn to see the world in a loving way. Cooperation and caring will be as "instinctive," as violence and aggression seem today.

•Our Godlike potentialities must be developed to the utmost. We must come to know the knower of facts—ourselves. Human-relations training, universal values, and cultivating higher consciousness must be a part of higher education.

•Our system of education has become somewhat fossilized by its current view of reality, a two-dimensional world of facts and figures. This view has so fragmented our wholeness, and has so increased separation, materiality, specialization and mechanical computerlike functioning, that we are in real danger of self-extermination.

•We need a path back to wholeness. We must be able to impart to our students an ability to tap the transcendent, the knowledge, fulfillment, and integrative power that lie dormant within.

•Too many have their imagination stifled by the standard educational process. We must find means to stimulate reverence, awe, and wonder—for a wildflower, the smooth skin of a frog, a shining star.

- We must renew an acquaintance with our natural mind, the field of all possibilities that intuits, imagines, and sings a song of joy. Rational thought must not be lost, but rather a new balance achieved.

- Teachers, by their own example, have a most glorious opportunity to instill love and character in their students. Better to encourage youth asking questions, than to stymie with ready-made answers. "I don't know" is an important first step to knowledge.

- Children learn better by praise than by blame, indifference, or the "rod." The most important motive for learning is love for parents or the teacher. You cannot praise a child too much or too well.

- Firmness or gentle confrontation, yes, but the withdrawal of love should never be used as punishment. The fear of rejection is a potent behavioral conditioner that can damage a child's development.

- Loving and stimulating day care and nursery schools, for children ages two to five, could do much for the emotional welfare of children and young parents. The earliest years of child development are the most crucial.

- The teaching and parenting of our young must be given a unique and special status. Parents and elementary school teachers are the creators of tomorrow's, more so than college professors, astronauts, or legislators.

DEVOTION

•As love deepens the heart becomes totally devoted; we surrender. Devotion is a natural culmination of our growth to inner fullness. The heart overflows with profound gratitude, appreciation, and love.

•Devotion to a person or some cause is not just for the sake of the object but for bringing out the very best in us. The spirit gains free reign and is uplifted. We surrender ourselves to the fullness of life and feel part of a larger flow.

•A fully devoted relationship is one of the noblest paths to an awakened consciousness. If devotion remains unabated, gradually the individual becomes purified. Unlovely conduct becomes impossible; the highest fulfillment dawns.

•In the love for the man/woman of our choice is contained the love for all men/women . . . for life itself . . . for the great oneness of all. A strong devotional relationship becomes the basis for service to family, community, church, and to society at large. Devotion can be focused on one's spouse; a great teacher; a noble cause, ideal, or principle; or God.

•God and good have more in common than just sharing the same letters. God calls us to the highest good. All goodness comes from God, and the bridge is love.

SERVICE

•Self-fulfillment does not lead to self-preoccupation or selfishness, as some might fear. On the contrary, it naturally leads to a growing concern for, and service to, others. No man has ever been thought of as selfish for pursuing his own good, but rather for neglecting the good of others.

•As consciousness expands, others become as dear to us as ourself, the universal self, which is each of us and all creation. Our talents, riches, and opportunities are seen as belonging not only to ourself but to all mankind.

•The best cure for worries, loneliness, and depression is to step outside of yourself by helping others. Lighten the burden of just one other person and your black clouds will dissipate, the sun will come shining through. Promoting the happiness and well-being of others is perhaps the greatest pleasure of all.

•There are so many people in need of help: blind students to be read to, shut-ins who need shopping done, older people who need their lawns mowed, hospitals in need of volunteers. Break down the barriers of your isolation. Get out there, you are needed.

•A loving person provides a help that is far greater than can be measured by external acts alone. His or her compassion reaches souls as well as bodies and inspires latent potentialities therein.

BROTHERLY LOVE

•Interdependence is an inherent part of our human condition. No one can make a sale, construct a bridge, ride an elevator, or run a farm without knowing this is so. Millions of people are involved in your daily use of services and products.

•Every thought, every action, affects our collective universe. Resolved: Let us love one another in fullness and spread grace all around. The welfare of each person is the welfare of all.

•Brother has fought brother seeing scarcity, while a joyous feast has been awaiting us. The fruits of cooperation with one another can bear a bountiful harvest, much greater than the crumbs gleaned through hostility and aggression.

•Every soul that touches yours, even if the contact be small, has some good to transfer to you—a new perspective, some little grace. Reach your hand out to another. Your loneliness can be ended that quickly.

•If you would seek to be a brother you must aim for differences with honor, power with humility, charity with respect. Whether or not your love is reciprocated pay homage to the essential sacredness of each and all.

•Brotherhood is more than a Sunday school word; it is our collective destiny. The very purpose of our lives is for us to grow together in love: when we can look our brother in the eye, I to I, and know that we are one.

JUSTICE

•In the soul of our personhood is a justice whose retribution is exacting and complete. A good action uplifts the doer; a negative deed and he instantly shrinks. He who lives by the highest principles gains the highest dignities and pleasures of life.

•Beyond man's law there is a cosmic law; you cannot escape remuneration for your actions, good and bad. As we sow, so shall we reap. All will be evened in the end, perhaps even by the end of the day. Strive to be fair in all of your transactions, material and emotional.

•There will never be enough laws as long as the world is filled with fear, hate, crime, and greed. Prejudice and injustice are societal stresses, the cure for which is not just passing laws but inspiring greater love and trust.

•Where there is love there is justice. Once a loving harmony has been established within the individual, he will automatically work for a more just and loving world. Compassion is to our personal love what mercy is to justice.

•Justice gains its strength from a deep passion for human rights, a belief in the dignity of man and the common good. Civil liberties are for those we like as well as dislike, those we agree and disagree with—a larger loving principle is in force.

•The tide is turning in human history, the power of organized evil is breaking down. Watergate was symptomatic of a larger catharsis, a national process of purification. Those in high places must now serve virtue or go asunder; justice will be served.

JOYOUS SIMPLICITY

•We Americans are 6 per cent of the global community but retain over one third of the global income. The other 94 per cent of mankind subsist on the other two thirds. To protect our excess share of the goodies, we Americans spend about twice as much per person on military defense as the annual per capita income of two thirds of the people of Earth. The bottom third of our global population (tries to) live on an annual per capita income of less than one hundred dollars per year.

•Simple living requires taking charge of our lives, returning material things to their proper role: serving human ends. By simplifying our own lives we can begin to take personal responsibility for solving the problems of overconsumption, maldistribution, and economic oppression.

•We have been putting the teaching of our profits ahead of those of our prophets. We must honor a new bottom line: The material must serve the spiritual so we all profit love.

•We are learning greed doesn't work. The malcontent and malnutrition of overconsumption plague many of us in the West while half the world starves. Social purpose, sharing, and global consciousness are fast growing in priority.

•New values are emerging placing inner before outer. By changing ourselves—our values, goals, and life style—we can profoundly change the world. As we become more whole our action will become more appropriate. We'll need less "externals" to be fulfilled.

•Voluntary simplicity† is the appropriate stance in the light of the lack suffered by two thirds of the human race. As a way of life this does not in any way mean penny-pinching, back-to-the-land, or poverty. On the contrary, it is a path to personal growth and abundance: outwardly simple but inwardly rich.

† Duane Elgin and Arnold Mitchell, "Voluntary Simplicity," *CoEvolution Quarterly*, No. 14, Summer 1977, pp. 4–19.

IMAGINE!

•There is nothing more powerful than an idea(s) whose time has come. Once our mind has been stretched it can never go back to its previous form. Transcending in thought and action expands our mind to the limit; a new world of possibilities opens.

•Cherish the music that murmurs in your heart. If you remain true to your highest ideals and steadfast upon the goal, your world of tomorrow will soon be built. The great opportunity to contribute is now, and if not by you, then whom?

•Aim high. Little plans have no capacity to stir the spirit. Failure is not a crime, but low aim is.

•Seize the time. A building, a poem, a career all begin with a stirring of the spirit; next a well-made plan. A journey of three thousand miles is begun by a single step, writes the ancient Chinese philosopher Lao-tzu. A tree that takes both arms to encircle grows from a tiny rootlet.

•Remember the words from George Bernard Shaw that were used by Ted Kennedy to eulogize his slain brother Robert: "Some men see things as they are and say, Why? I dream things that never were and say, Why not?" Noble dreams give rise to great human beings, and the best yet remains to be done.

•Let's all agree to take a half day off, turn off every phone, silence the hustle-bustle of our activity, and meet in a secluded setting, perhaps a forest or an orange grove. Better yet, and certainly more practical, let's all meet inside, in the silent chambers of our soul. Perhaps then our deepest yearnings will emerge: Why we are living, what's it all about?

• Love one another and all glory will come to the earth. This is a most ancient and venerated teaching, but now its time has come. The possibility of a society based on love, truth, beauty, and justice is not based upon romantic notions, but the collective evolution of our human spirit.

A REALIZED SOCIETY

•History records the dream of a realized society—creative, peaceful, productive, and just—in every generation. Such a society is possible, but it can only arise from the minds, hearts, and behavior of a fully functioning citizenry.

•It has been all too easy for us to blame governments, rising bureaucracies, the military-industrial complex, and ineffectual schools for our existing social problems. Our institutions are a reflection of each one of us. We get the leadership we deserve.

•Tapping our inner wellspring of love can not only produce happy individuals, but transform our failing professions and institutions. The doctor who loves, serves healing. The lawyer who loves, serves justice. The teacher who loves, serves education.

•Does peace of mind and a loving heart negate your social activism? As you become more accepting and imperturbable will you passively accept exploitation, prejudice, and pollution? Most assuredly, no.

•Responsible social action develops as a natural consequence of increased care and concern for others. Rage and frustration are not prerequisites for building a better world. On the contrary, these may add to the fear and animosity which already exist.

•Favor positivity. Only a small percentage of a population, perhaps one or two per cent, need increase their inner ease, harmony, and values for the effect to become manifest on a larger social scale. Love is highly contagious; its effect may be incurable!

IT COULD ALL BEGIN WITH YOU

Since true foundation cannot fail
But holds as good as new
Many a worshipful son shall hail
A father who lived true.
Realized in one man, fitness has its rise;
Realized in a family, fitness multiplies;
Realized in a village, fitness gathers weight;
Realized in a country, fitness becomes great;
Realized in the world, fitness fills the skies
And thus the fitness of one man
You find in the family he began,
You find in the village that accrued,
You find in the country that ensued,
You find in the world's whole multitude.
How do I know this integrity?
Because it could all begin in me.

—Lao-tzu

TOWARD A NEW AGE

•While the white dove of peace inspires us, war has repeatedly darkened our path. Human beings have slaughtered over one hundred million of our fellow men and women in this century alone. The problem of war has proven so intractable that some theorists suggest destructive aggression is innately a part of man.

•Evolution of the heart and mind must catch up and overtake the rule of muscle and brute force. Let's not forget the specter of a nuclear holocaust. Our weapons have gotten so monstrous, that we must seek to avoid a planetary doomsday. Larger problems—the environment, dwindling resources, the energy crisis, world economy—are pressing. Détente must give rise to true affection and cooperation. We must learn to love one another or die.

•The solution to world peace lies in solving the problem of individual peace. As is emphasized in the UNESCO charter, "Wars start in the minds of men." It is the collective screams and sighs of unhappy people, that ultimately gives rise to the cry of war.

•Laws, armies, treaties, spying satellites, and nuclear inspection will never end the problem of war. For a nation as well as for an individual, external defenses can never make up for a lack of internal security. Real security is not to be gained from building ever larger weapon systems, but by generating more love and peace in the world. A lasting peace is not to be found in an analysis of world power, but in the hearts of men.

•There is cause for optimism and hope. Love occupies a more important place in world affairs than any prior age in history.

The use of slavery, torture, or cruelty is more abhorrent than ever before. A collective disdain for coercion and mass murder (put bluntly, that's what war is), cannot lie far behind.

•There are things each of us can do; a peaceful world begins with you. Above all, generate more peace and love in your own heart. You will naturally radiate an influence of peace and harmony for the world.

•It is easier to love people who think, act, and look like you. Start loving those people who disagree with you, who are very different from yourself. See the unity that underlies vast differences. "Love thine enemy," for even your enemy is a part of you.

•Let's stop lauding assassins, mass murderers, and hijackers. What we put attention on in our lives tends to grow stronger. We need to emphasize more the good news. Recognizing the goodness in others and the world will help the goodness thrive.

•Just as the paranoid individual wastes approximately 80 per cent of his life energy on fear and mistrust, so we have collectively been putting about 80 per cent of our resources into weaponry of war. Let's channel more of our individual and national resources into building bridges of mutual hope, cooperation, and understanding.

•For peace we must raise our collective consciousness, always starting with ourselves. "As long as you see your fellow man as a being essentially to be feared, mistrusted, hated and destroyed, there cannot be peace on earth. Where there is a deep, simple, all-embracing love of man, of the created world of living and inanimate things, then there will be respect for life, for freedom, for truth, for justice," so wrote Thomas Merton.‡

‡ Thomas Merton, "The Christian in Crisis: Reflections on the Moral Climate of the 1960's," in *Thomas Merton on Peace*. McCall Publishing Co., New York, 1971.

TRANSFORMATION AT THE SPEED OF LOVE

•Nature is supporting the growth of love in today's world; we just need to lend ourselves to the process. To the degree that more universal love is being mirrored in the hearts and minds of the people, a global transformation, a new age, is at hand.

•Great epochs in social progress are visible throughout history, but few people in the past have been privileged to recognize a great transformation at its earliest stage. The acceleration of progress in today's world is allowing us to witness immense social transformation in our lifetime, from global communication to space age travel.

•We now have the technology to master not only outer space, but perhaps more importantly, inner space as well. With the systematic and widespread application of programs to develop our latent human potentialities, there is every reason to believe we could achieve the dawning of a new age of beauty, justice, and joy.

•Our new age will not be constructed by revolution, but by evolution—the growth of consciousness. A loving person is able to accept the world as it is, while he simultaneously works to improve it. He works rapidly for constructive change, but without exceeding the speed limit. The future is built on the best of the past and present.

•The real transformation must occur first on the level of consciousness, infusing our thoughts and actions with love. By transforming ourselves we spontaneously transform our culture. As consciousness evolves, institutional and historical change will follow.

•Anything that is false, unjust, or impure withers away in the face of a rising wave of love. There is no need to abolish or actively destroy anything. The light of knowledge immediately dispels the darkness.

•The awakened person sees all social change from a larger, cosmic perspective. Human history, including its wars, trials, and tribulations, is the story of consciousness in search of greater satisfaction. We humans have only been around for a veritable second of cosmic history. A social order based on love is possible, but it will take time. A firm patience is necessary; we are still in our infancy.

•Certainly the world is full of dread and danger, but also promise and possibility. Planetary events (education, interdependence, transportation, communication) are, in a sense, conspiring to inspire us to recognize our oneness amid diversity.

•Love/happiness is even more infectious than its polar opposite, anger/fear. It's just that we haven't given love the full light of day. Through our own self-renewal, we can fulfill the American dream: "Novus Ordo Seclorum," a new order for the ages. Ten, twenty, one hundred years from now, the historical transition now under way will be obvious to all.

•Seen from this larger perspective, one can fully enjoy the transformation. One comes to realize that the founding principle of the universe is love, and that the fulfillment of each and every one of us is, in the long run, inevitable. All negativity and temporary sorrows pale before this transcendental contentment.

•Let's not get too abstract, for it all begins with you. It's a matter of your growing, sharing, and transcending. I wish you love and joy.

BIBLIOGRAPHY

Bloomfield, Harold, and Kory, Robert, *Happiness: The TM Program, Psychiatry, and Enlightenment.* New York: Simon & Schuster, 1976.

——*The Holistic Way to Health and Happiness.* New York: Simon & Schuster, 1978.

Colgrove, Melba, Bloomfield, Harold, and McWilliams, Peter, *How to Survive the Loss of a Love.* New York: Simon & Schuster, 1976.

Fromm, Erich, *The Art of Loving.* New York: Bantam Books, 1956.

——*The Ability to Love.* New York: Pocket Books, 1965.

Gibran, Kahlil, *The Prophet.* New York: Alfred A. Knopf, 1976.

Inkeles, Gordon, and Todris, Murray, with photographs by R. Foothorap, *The Art of Sensual Massage.* New York: Simon & Schuster, 1972.

James, William, *The Varieties of Religious Experience.* London: Longmans, Green & Co., 1929.

Kubler-Ross, Elizabeth, *On Death and Dying.* New York: Macmillan Co., 1969.

Maharishi Mahesh Yogi, *Love and God.* New York: MIU Press, 1976.

Maslow, Abraham, *Toward a Psychology of Being.* New York: D. Van Nostrand Co., 1968.

Merrel-Wolff, Frank, *Pathways Through to Space*. New York: Warner Books, 1976.

Merton, Thomas, "The Christian in Crisis: Reflections on the Moral Climate of the 1960's," in *Thomas Merton on Peace*. New York: McCall Publishing Co., 1971.

Montagu, Ashley, *The Direction of Human Development*, rev. ed. New York: Hawthorne Books, Inc., 1970.

Moody, Raymond, *Life After Life*. New York: Bantam Books, 1975.

Ray, Sandra, *I Deserve Love*. Millbrae, California: Les Femmes Publishing Company, 1976.

Zitko, Howard, *Tantra Yoga*. Tucson, Arizona: World University Press, 1975.

ACKNOWLEDGMENTS

This book is an attempt to make available the best teachings on love, both ancient and modern. I wish to express my profound gratitude to all the great teachers on love, who I have drawn upon, and who have greatly enriched my life and thought. Erich Fromm, Ashley Montagu, Abraham Maslow, and Kahlil Gibran provided constant inspiration. The author owes a very deep and special gratitude to the teachings of Maharishi Mahesh Yogi.

Special thanks to Robert Kory and Peter McWilliams for their personal and professional influence upon me, and for their contribution to some of the ideas in this book. I am most grateful to Barbara Carpenter, John Edmister, Cherylyn Davis, Mike and Donna Fletcher, and Ali and Sibyl Rubottom for suggestions and editorial comments.

My appreciation to Karen Van Westering, my editor, for her support, inputs, and kindly association. Paul Sutherland significantly improved the flow of the manuscript. Amy Kabatznick, Nora Stern, and Mary Ann Huening, stand out for their typing and assistance.

In memory of Betty Lewis, who, in living and dying, expanded my horizons of love. Special thanks to my father, mother, and sister, friends and associates, and all those who have helped me to experientially learn my lessons on love.